I0156879

# Stay Here with Me

# Stay Here with Me

## Memoir of an American Family

Monica Berriz-Ocon

E. L. Marker
Salt Lake City

E. L. Marker, an imprint of WiDō Publishing
Salt Lake City, Utah
widopublishing.com

Copyright © 2020 by Monica Berriz-Ocon

All rights reserved. No part of this book may be reproduced or transmitted in any form or by any means, electronic or mechanical, including photocopying, recording, or by any information storage and retrieval system without the written consent of the publisher.

Cover photo: 1959 Key Biscayne, Florida, Stay here with me.
Cover design by Steven Novak
Book design by Marny K. Parkin

ISBN 978-1-947966-41-3

Dedicated to Mamá, *mi angel.*

And to all the victims of the 2017 Northern California fires.

"Fire has always been and, seemingly, will always remain, the most terrible of the elements."

—Harry Houdini

# La Familia Berriz

My parents met in the spring of 1954; my father was thirteen, and my mother was twelve. They lived in the same Havana neighborhood, just blocks from each other, but attended different schools: my father at the local public school, my mother at a Catholic school for girls run by nuns. My father, Armando Berriz, was the catcher on his school baseball team, which was coached by Cookie Rojas' father. As children, Cookie and my father played sandlot ball together; Cookie pitched, my father caught. Cookie would go on to have a major league career in America and become a star player for the Phillies and Royals. The school team that year was in the hunt for a championship, which meant the entire neighborhood was rooting for these boys.

One weekend the team's shortstop, Ignacio, a boy who knew everyone and was always surrounded by girls, telephoned my father from a house near the beach. He said, "Hey, Armando, you should come down here. There are lots of girls from the neighborhood."

My father told Ignacio he couldn't make it down to the beach, so Ignacio passed the phone to the girls. "Here, talk to Armando! Get him to come down here!"

The first girl squealed into the phone for a few seconds before handing it off to the next girl who similarly squealed and passed the phone off to another. In those days in Cuba, it didn't take much for even innocent interactions between a boy and girl to draw the attention of protective parents or well-meaning neighbors. The way my father tells it, that phone passed so quickly between the first few girls, it was as if they believed that holding it any longer with a boy on the other end would cause a scandal. Then the girl who would become my mother got on the line. Even at that age, she was unafraid of talking to people, and she formally introduced herself. My father, who was too young to have had any experience with girls, didn't have much to say to twelve-year-old Carmen Caldentey, so he asked the obvious questions: was she enjoying the beach? Where did she go to school? Where did she live?

My mother answered politely, and, according to my father, communicated a confidence and poise that fascinated him. The conversation probably didn't last a minute, but my father knew within seconds that he wanted to meet this Carmen girl who lived nearby. A week later, he knocked on her door at the ridiculously inappropriate hour of seven a.m.

Mrs. Caldentey answered the door, and young Armando Berriz presented himself to the woman who stared down at him.

"Hi Carmela, I mean M-Mrs. Caldentey. I've come to visit with Carmencita, is she available?"

Carmela, unamused and unimpressed by this boy's request to speak with her daughter, responded, "She's sleeping. Go wait for her over there, on that stoop. She'll awake shortly," and she closed the door.

Undaunted, Armando took a seat on the stoop and waited.

How long he was left sitting on the stoop, he doesn't remember, but eventually, Carmen came to the door. Standing there before him in the morning light, she seemed shyer and more diffident than she had been on the phone, no doubt in part because she had curlers in her hair and suspected her mother was very disapproving of this young man's unexpected appearance at their home. Armando presented himself again and told her how much he had enjoyed speaking with her on the phone. Then, having accomplished his mission, he went on his way. Though Carmen had undoubtedly sparked his imagination on the phone, meeting her in person left him feeling somewhat indifferent about the whole thing.

A week later, at a neighborhood party, Armando noticed Carmen sitting on a sofa. To be polite more than anything else, he sat down next to her, and, in this more neutral environment, without her mother hovering inches away, Carmen Caldentey and Armando Berriz had their first genuine conversation. My father doesn't remember what they talked about, but he remembers being entranced by how well this young woman spoke, her presence, the sound of her voice, and her poise, all of which was far beyond what he had observed before in any girl, or woman for that matter. My mother remembers being charmed by his earnestness, forthright manners, and sincere attention.

It had been only two weeks since they had spoken on the phone as strangers, but following this conversation at a neighborhood party, Armando and Carmen never entertained the idea of ever loving anyone else.

Thankfully for them, neighborhood parties were common in those days, and they had ample opportunities to find themselves in the same place at the same time without arousing too much adult attention. Carmen was an excellent dancer, Armando a terrible one, but that didn't stop him from following her around the party circuit and dancing with her whenever he could. One song that especially inspired him to keep up with my mother on the dancefloor was Jo Stafford's "You Belong to Me." It was the song they were dancing to the first time they kissed, on the terrazzo of her parents' house.

Armando was keenly aware he had competition for Carmen's attention. She looked older and seemed more mature than her age, and he noticed other boys and even men were constantly looking at her. Some stared. The boldest would approach her the way a cat might stalk a bird. One afternoon they were walking together down the street from her house to get an ice cream when the older brother of one of his schoolmates drove up behind them in a gleaming Hudson. The older boy slowed down as he approached them from behind, stuck his elbow out the window, and said to her, "That little boy's too young for you."

Armando felt a flush of anger of a kind he hadn't experienced before. His pride was hurt, but he was also humiliated and confused that people failed to see what was so obvious to him—that he and Carmen were destined for one another and had been from the day of the party.

He wanted to thrash the boy in the Hudson. He wanted Carmen to call the boy a stupid lowlife. Neither of these things happened because that's not who they were, nor how they had been raised, but it was an indelible moment for him. He told me later it was then he realized that until he and Carmen were married, there would be competition for her attention coming from all sides and underminers lurking everywhere. He also decided that he would never again let that make him angry, jealous, or petty. Instead, he would become the only man worthy of Carmen Caldentey.

MY GRANDPARENTS ON BOTH SIDES FELT MY PARENTS WERE too young to be so serious, but the reservations were especially strong on my father's side, where the possibility of their son being in a failed relationship was especially painful to contemplate since they were in a failed marriage themselves. Failed marriages stretched back to my father's grandfather, Luis Miro Berriz, a big-shot civil engineer who had lived with his wife, America Camejo, and their children in a large home at the edge of the city with a library and carriage house. For reasons unknown, Luis Miro Berriz divorced his wife during the 1930s, creating a scandal that left a permanent stain on the family's reputation as well as their fortune. My great-grandmother and her children continued to live in the house her husband had built, but there was no longer a carriage, nor any horses, nor any expectation of having a car.

America Camejo would never remarry, and the stigma of her divorce attached itself to her sons. None of her boys had a steady job, which wasn't all that unusual in Cuba at the time, but their poor reputations sapped any ambitions they may have once had, and they made little effort to find work. Her daughter, Bertha Miro Camejo, was a great beauty and would go on to win a local beauty pageant. This gave her opportunities her brothers didn't have, and when she met Armando Alberto Berriz Molina at a social club, everyone assumed that she, the beauty queen, and Armando, a star athlete, would be a perfect match. Being young and ignorant, they thought their elders knew something they didn't, and they ended up marrying.

My grandparents' relationship deteriorated quickly, and my father cannot remember a time growing up when his parents weren't constantly arguing. Their arguments might have been driven by my grandmother's deep depression, which drove her to seek electroshock therapy when my father was around nine years old. At the time, he didn't realize what that meant when she told him she was being treated, but he saw she became withdrawn, morose, and mistrustful. In a desperate bid to fix their failing marriage, my grandparents pursued marriage counseling. The practice was in its infancy and strongly influenced by the Catholic church, so perhaps it is no surprise they were encouraged to have more children. The results seem to illustrate their desperation: my aunt was born nine years after my father, and my uncle followed seven years later.

WHEN HE TURNED TWELVE YEARS OLD, MY GRANDFATHER gave my dad a Daisy BB gun for his birthday. It was his prized possession as a boy, and having it solidified his appreciation for outdoor adventures, a passion that remained a constant throughout his life. He'd go fishing and hunting, play baseball in the street, or create elaborate amusements for himself on the beach. These adventures provided him with an escape from his unhappy parents and a sense of freedom that he came to relish. The Jardín Zoológico de la Habana, in the center of the city, provided plenty of diversion for a young boy with a BB gun.

There were always small animals roaming around outside the walls of the zoo: rodents mostly, along with an assortment of stray dogs and cats. One afternoon my father was tracking small game around the streets near the zoo, occasionally squeezing off a shot, when a neighbor with a gentler spirit toward animals called the police on him. When the patrol car arrived, the officers had no problem finding him. He was the only kid running through the bushes with a BB gun. They picked him up and took him home.

When my grandmother saw a police car pull up outside her home on a late afternoon that summer, she was more than a little nervous. Havana was a tense place in 1955, and it was commonplace to hear about people being picked up by the authorities and not returning home. She watched as a policeman got out of the car, holding her son's Daisy BB gun in hand. My father, fourteen years old at the time, looked out the window toward the house with an expression of defiance that worried my grandmother more than the police.

My grandmother, already emotionally withdrawn at this point, was still aware of what was happening inside the country. There were few opportunities for many young people in Batista's Cuba, and they grew restless and resentful of the regime and its authorities. She heard lots of stories about parents discovering their children had become radicalized with communist and revolutionary ideas. She always worried an unfortunate run-in with the police might set her strong-willed and stubborn son in the wrong direction, and now here he was in the back of their car.

When the police left, she looked her son in the eye and said, "Sometimes I'm scared for you, Armando. I don't know what you're thinking."

"What do you mean?"

"Stay out of trouble."

My father looked around the room. It was comfortably furnished, but it was dark and quiet. It held no signs of life or family. Like the rest of the house, there was no sense that anyone lived there. It was just a place that sheltered them from the elements, where they ate and slept, but didn't live. He looked at the bookcases set against the wall. Some cobwebs were visible between the tops of the books and the bottoms of the shelves. He wondered how long it had been since anyone else in the house had touched one of those beautiful old books.

"Mamá, I'm not in trouble. I was just enjoying myself. Just living. I'll be okay."

"There are a lot of bad things happening," she said.

"I know," he said, "but they're not going to happen to me. You'll see."

My father took away two things from that day: he was always going to be a hunter, and he would never let fear shape his future.

# La Familia Caldentey

MY MOTHER WAS BORN ONE YEAR, ONE MONTH, AND ONE week after my father. Her mother, Carmela, was Cuban. Her father, Juan, was a Spaniard born in Mallorca who moved to Cuba because he didn't want any part of the Spanish Civil War.

Juan Caldentey knew how to leverage connections, and after scraping by for a few years, he partnered with some friends to purchase a struggling bar. The bar was a success, so they purchased another bar together which was even more successful. Juan Caldentey was not satisfied with being a partner. Once he'd saved enough money, he bought a run-down, three-story hotel near the train station, the Monserrate, which he refurbished. He brought a Spanish sensibility to the hotel. When it came to food, he never bought mayonnaise or baked goods. He made them himself, and whatever he made was superior to anything available from the local stores or bakeries. When it came to entertaining business clients, he never tried to dazzle them by taking them to a casino full of Americans. He would make them a meal they could not get in America, or anywhere else in Havana for that matter. That was the way Mallorcans did things. It set his establishment apart from the competition and contributed to its success. It also set his family apart. Though Juan Caldentey and his wife Maria del Carmen Andrade Cepero would find success in Havana, they would never call it home.

My maternal grandparents had very firm ideas on how they wanted to raise their children, which included frequent trips to Mallorca to absorb Spanish culture and family life. My mother remembers her father making homemade meringue, taking her to markets, teaching her how to buy olive oil, and how to identify quality leather. Near the end of these trips, the entire family would get dressed up and take a ride on the Ferrocarril de Soller, making the same day trip on the old-fashioned narrow-gauge train Juan Caldentey had ridden with his parents when he was a child.

Maria del Carmen, known to her friends and family as Carmela, made her daughter's dresses for her. She would explain to my mother how she made them, why she chose the materials she used for them, the effects of different sewing techniques, how to appreciate fashion and, especially, how to identify quality. Clothes did not have to be expensive nor have designer labels, but they must be well-made, stylish, flattering, and always appropriate to the occasion.

My mother was sent to charm school. She was fluent in English and French by the time she finished high school. When the family gathered for dinner, they discussed the food they were eating— where it came from, its nutritional value, its cultural history, and perhaps most important, why the food was prepared and served the way it was. Family dinner was not only a time to eat; it was a time to teach their children about culture, heritage, and how to be in the world. All this my grandparents did for their daughter, which gave her an elegance and self-confidence beyond her years. I'm sure that was part of what captivated many of the boys who expressed an interest in her, including my father. I know it captivated me as a child.

Carmen Caldentey may have been tall, willowy, and cosmopolitan, but she was hardly weak. She played volleyball from a young age, and her hands and arms were strong. She pushed herself hard and trained for hours, and while still in high school, she qualified for the women's Cuban Olympic volleyball team. She remembers her excitement when she found out she had made the team. She was so excited, in fact, that my normally poised and elegant mother began jumping up and down in a circle, overcome with joy. She remembers her coach saying, "You earned this, Carmencita. *¡Excelente! ¡Pase, set, remate! La medalla de oro* will be yours! I know it."

Her dream was shattered as soon as the coach told her parents. They refused to let her participate. They had so many rules about what was and wasn't appropriate and acceptable when she was growing up. The Olympics was the most ambitious, certainly, but it wasn't an exception. The most important thing, however, was her relationship with Armando Berriz, regardless of how hard her parents tried to separate them.

But oh, how they tried. In the beginning, they said she was too young to be so serious about a boy, and they would take her to Europe for months on end to keep her away from Armando. When she was a little older, they insisted on introducing their daughter to young men from Spanish families with more status than the Berrizes. They refused to socialize with Armando's parents, neither accepting invitations to meals nor offering any. They made their displeasure known in every way they could. None of it made a difference. Even when the Berrizes emigrated to the US, and the Caldenteys stayed in Cuba, neither distance nor time diminished the bond Carmen and Armando had from the very beginning.

My father would often say my mother was the least-Cuban Cuban woman he'd ever met. That meant a lot of different things. Growing up, the women my father knew were simpler and not as urbane as my mother. They also lacked my mother's drive and confidence. That confidence manifested itself in a fearlessness coupled with an adventurous spirit that would have been rare anywhere, but in my father's world, it was very rare. This quality, also shared by my father, was one reason my parents persisted in seeing each other at such a young age even in the face of the sternest warnings from their elders. My parents were not rebellious people by nature, but they were also not unquestioningly compliant either. Even growing up in a Latin family during the fifties, in a culture where the teachings of the church dictated that children be respectful of authority and follow the rules, didn't deter them from following through on something once they had committed to it.

Once my mother's parents discovered they could not stop their daughter from seeing thirteen-year-old Armando, they enlisted family members to follow Carmen and Armando wherever they went. Chaperoning, they called it. On days when Carmela or one of her sisters was unavailable, Carmen's five-year-old brother Juan would assume the role. Armando and Carmen soon realized the obvious advantages of this. If they ever needed Juan to turn his head and look the other way while they snuck a kiss or two, he was easily bribed with treats, car rides, and movies complete with popcorn and candy. Whenever possible, they planned their dates so Juan would chaperone.

When Armando Berriz was fourteen, his parents sent him to the Manlius school, a military academy in upstate New York. It was 1955, Batista had dissolved the Cuban parliament, and they wanted to be sure their son would not become a revolutionary. I'm sure they also thought sending him to the United States would put an end to his relationship with Carmen. In this, they were wrong. He wrote and mailed Carmen a letter every single day he was away.

By 1957, his parents had also emigrated to the United States and were living in Pennsylvania. He was finishing his senior year at Manlius and had been accepted to a university on the east coast. He spent his summer before college at his parents' home in Pennsylvania, and the day before he was to head back east, he paid a visit to the Mother Superior of the Handmaidens and told her his plans. He may have been willful, but he had an abiding faith in God and in the Catholic church.

When he told the Mother Superior his college plans, her response was immediate and unequivocal. "No, no, Armando," she said. "You cannot go to that school."

"But I'm leaving tomorrow. Why not?"

"Because you have to go to a Catholic university."

Before he could protest any further, she waved him off, picked up the phone, and dialed. Covering the mouthpiece, she looked up and asked, "What do you want to study, Armando?"

"Engineering," he replied.

"Father Klekotka, please," she said into the phone.

When Father Klekotka came to the phone, she said, "Father, this is Mother Mary Brennan at Handmaids of the Sacred Heart. I have a boy here from Cuba who wants to be an engineer, and it's important to me and his family that he go to a Catholic school, so I'm sending him to you personally. He will be there tomorrow."

The next day his parents drove him to Villanova to meet Father Klekotka, and at age sixteen, Armando Berriz was admitted to Villanova University. Photos taken during his first year at Villanova show him sitting on an unmade bed littered with empty beer cans. He sports a pompadour, a fat cigar in his mouth, and a Clark Gable grin. Any fear his mother had about her son becoming a revolutionary must have dissolved during his freshman year at Villanova.

Meanwhile, my parents continued to write to one another on an almost daily basis. Neither family encouraged the relationship though they could no longer use their age as a reason to break it off. "Why are you so attached to a girl still living in Cuba?" my father's parents would ask. "Why not an American girl? Fewer problems, you know." They were relentless in the endeavor, firm in the belief an American girl would help their son assimilate into US culture and, eventually, achieve greater success there than he could with a Cuban woman at his side. Over 1,000 miles and an ocean away, my mother's family pressured her to seek someone different, preferably a Spanish boy. When either one of them became discouraged by the persistent opposition to their relationship, the other would say, *"¡Pase, set, remate!"* Bump, set, spike! They had taken the phrase from my mother's volleyball experience. It was their private code for "You can do this!" and they continued to use it throughout their life to encourage each other in challenging situations. My mother would say it to my father before an important meeting with clients, or when he was trying to figure out some complicated business deal. He would say it to her when she had a particularly delicate situation to negotiate at work. When my siblings and I were older, they would send us off to school on test days with a hug, a smile, and a *"¡Pase, set, remate!"* Bump, set, spike!

WHO KNOWS WHAT MIGHT HAVE HAPPENED IF THE CUBAN authorities had not knocked on Juan Caldentey's door in the spring of 1961 and told him that his children were going to be sent to an educational school in the countryside. Within months, he sent his wife and children to live in Miami, and by late August, Juan Caldentey walked away from everything he had spent years building in Cuba and joined them. It was late August 1961. By this time, the Berrizes had moved from Pennsylvania to Florida, joining the growing middle class of Cuban exiles. Once again, the Berriz and Caldentey families were living in the same city but living very different lives. The Caldentey family never managed to achieve the success they'd had in Cuba. Juan Caldentey left nearly all his money in Cuba, and in a city teeming with exiles, competition for work was fierce. His wife Carmela spoke no English, which rendered her virtually unemployable. Juan spoke limited English, just enough to land him the occasional odd job. He took whatever he could find. It was up to their daughter to help the family make ends meet; she landed a job with the Chamber of Commerce by exaggerating her work experience with her father's hotel.

As Juan and Carmela struggled, their attitude toward their daughter's relationship with Armando changed. During his senior year, Armando had interviewed and gotten a job with Cal-Trans, the state agency responsible for building and maintaining California's transportation systems. He would start as soon as he graduated at the end of his spring term in 1962. Juan and Carmela could see their future son-in-law was ambitious, intelligent, and had a stable future ahead of him. They knew that attending Villanova had been a financial strain on the Berriz family, and they had watched Armando draw a kind of strength out of his family's troubles that had pushed him to succeed. They respected him for this. They also recognized that their daughter's relationship with Armando provided opportunity for a better life than what Miami could offer. They allowed their son Juan, now twelve years old, to chaperone them with increasing regularity, a tacit sign of approval that didn't go unnoticed by the couple. They spoke openly of marriage and even discussed the idea of Carmen's parents following them to California.

To my parents, that time in Miami was when all the obstacles that had threatened to keep them apart began to crumble. It was as if the world finally understood what they had known for years: they belonged together, and they would be together.

# La Familia Caldentey-Berriz

My parents were married in Florida in June of 1962, and immediately after the ceremony, they packed their belongings in a wedding gift from my father's parents, a '57 Chevy Impala. It would take them about four days to reach their new home in Glendale, California, where my father would start his job at CalTrans.

They knew next to nothing about California, but when it had come time to decide where to live, my mother had taken out a map, spread it out on the kitchen table of her parents' home, found the area her husband would be working, closed her eyes, and planted her index finger on the map.

Glendale.

The place sounded idyllic, so that is where they moved, sight unseen.

Her brother had been astonished.

"It sounds like a lovely place," was all she said.

Driving across the western United States, especially at that time, wasn't easy. Cars would break down or overheat with regularity. Coming into California, in a town called Needles, the fuel pump in their Impala gave out. As they sat in the repair shop waiting for their car, they marveled at how much different the West was from Florida: gas prices were double, things were more expensive in general, but the wide-openness of the terrain especially captured their imaginations.

My parents bought their first house in 1962 with a down payment of $2,000, which they borrowed from my mother's parents. The house was on North Isabel Street, just south of the mountains in Glendale. It was a comfortable, Spanish-style bungalow with three bedrooms and two bathrooms. From the front yard, the southeast end of the Verdugo Hills was visible to the north, and downtown Glendale to the south. I was born there, as were both my siblings: Carmen, my older sister, and Armando Jr., my younger brother. My mother's parents lived nearby in the San Fernando Valley with Juan. My mother, who had been "chaperoned" by him, now enlisted him to help with everything from babysitting to painting.

My father was twenty-one years old when he started working at CalTrans. At that time, the company had a policy that one couldn't obtain an engineering license before the age of twenty-five. He was working on a bridge that crossed a channel in San Diego. One day he told the project manager that his bridge was too long, and they could shorten it by putting a pier in the middle of the channel. The manager initially disagreed, but my father persisted, pointing out the agency could save millions of dollars by changing the bridge's design, and he showed the manager mathematically how it could be done. The design of the bridge was changed, and the higher-ups in CalTrans took notice of their bright young assistant engineer who had figured out how to shorten the span of a bridge by a hundred feet and save the agency millions in dollars and man-hours in the process. From then on, even though he hadn't yet obtained his license, and he wasn't given a raise, my father worked on increasingly high profile and complex projects.

In those days, most people stayed at an organization their entire career, but not my father. He made CalTrans a stepping stone to a larger career. As soon as he obtained his engineering license, he left CalTrans to work for a company that made construction products. His professional peers and even some family members thought he was insane to leave. At his new company, he helped develop new products and eventually went into managing projects and people.

While my father built a successful business career, my mother made a career of her own as the secretary for Alan Wayne, the lobbyist for United Airlines. Anyone who wanted to reach her boss would have to go through her, and she established excellent relationships with most of the state's leading politicians and their girlfriends. She loved to tell the story about a US congressman who had told his secretary to send his wife and children on vacation to Disneyworld in Florida, so he could "canoodle with his girlfriend." It turns out his secretary, disapproving of the congressman's behavior, had sent his wife and kids to Disneyland in California instead. The congressman had thought he'd have most of the day to say goodbye to the girlfriend before his family returned from vacation, so when he found out he had an hour at most, he called Alan Wayne's office for help in getting his mistress on a plane and out of town in a hurry. Time was ticking, and in desperation, the congressman explained why he needed to change this woman's ticket. My mother listened to his desperate plight, but she had to cover the phone's mouthpiece to prevent the congressman from hearing her laughter. My mother could never refuse anyone genuinely in need of help, but she couldn't abide philanderers, and in her mind, the worst kind of man was one who used his position for illicit gains and pleasures. She believed power should support families, not undermine them. She let the congressman talk for some time while feigning sympathy, then told him he just missed the chance to change the woman's ticket by a minute, and there was absolutely nothing she could do to help him. The mistress would need to find another way out of town. It was like she was Juno, protectress of marriage and the family. She was also immensely discreet. When she shared stories from her work, she never shared specific details that would embarrass someone. No one ever knew the name of that congressman but her.

My mother's integrity and discretion contributed significantly to her career success and to our family's income. In the summer of 1976, we moved to a larger house in Glendale on Mountain Street, which in time would become the hub for our entire family. I clearly remember it was sweltering during the weekend we moved because my siblings and I complained about it non-stop as we hauled our belongings up eighty-six steps to our bedrooms. The Mountain Street house was a beautiful Spanish-style home just a couple of blocks up the street from our house on Isabel, but it felt a world away because of its incredible view. From the front yard, one could see all of downtown Glendale and beyond as if standing on top of a glorious peak. I was twelve years old when we moved to that house, and I still remember that hot day, standing in the front yard, looking down at the city beneath us and feeling like my family was on top of the world.

In a sense, we were. We were a typical family, maybe doing a bit better than some, not as well as others, but we were happy. I had fights with my sister. My sister and I both complained about my brother. My brother complained about my sister and me. We played in the street. We chased the ice cream man. We went to the movies. We followed the Dodgers. We listened to Peter Frampton and the Eagles on the radio in our rooms and salsa and disco records on the stereo during the adults' parties. We played board games during our evenings at home, and on camping trips, I especially loved playing a little one-to-one Scrabble with my mother on weekend afternoons. Scrabble was my mom's favorite game, and she was an expert, seriously competitive player. She must have memorized every two-letter word in English, most words beginning with a "z," and a ridiculous number containing an "x." One challenged her at their peril, and she would only accept the challenge if it included a penalty in the form of something affectionate or delicious. As a family, we were blessed, and we knew it. We didn't feel special in any way, just grateful. God was good, and He was good to us.

One day, my father learned that a schoolmate of his had died in Miami. "Do you remember that day when that guy driving the Hudson said I was too young for you?" he asked my mother.

My mother paused and finally said, "Yes. I do. Why?"

"His younger brother was a friend of mine in school. He just died."

"Your friend or the jerk in the car?"

"He was more of an acquaintance than a friend."

"I've never forgotten that day," she said.

"Neither have I, but tell me why you've never forgotten it."

"Your restraint impressed me."

"It was hard."

"I know."

"But that day, the jerk in the Hudson, it taught me something," he said.

"What was that?"

"That I would do whatever it took to be with you. That there had to be an 'us.' No one was ever going to take that from me."

"You knew it that day? What took you so long?"

My father laughed. "I knew it the day we met. But that day, that moment, crystalized it in my mind in a way I couldn't quite articulate until that moment."

"If I'd known you were so slow, I might have had second thoughts."

"You've never had a second thought in your life."

That was true, and hearing him say that made me realize just how well my parents knew one another.

I watched as he took my mother in his arms and brought her close to him.

# La Familia Berriz-Ocon

THE TWELVE-YEAR-OLD ME COULD NOT HAVE SEEN THAT I would get married and divorced in my twenties, raise my daughter as a single parent, and only later in life, in my forties, meet the man who could make my life everything I had hoped for back in 1976. The road to happiness is a circuitous one, full of twists, turns, and occasional dead-ends. It requires no small measure of faith, but the faith will be rewarded, even if it takes a long time. A very long time.

I left Arielle's father when our daughter was only six months old. He was a good man, is a good man, and he's been a marvelous father to Arielle, but in marrying him, I had chosen to live someone else's life. I was living the life my mother led—staying at home until I got married, then having children so that I could build my life around my family. I had watched my older sister follow that path, so when I was ready to leave my parents' home, the only path I considered was marriage and moving into my husband's home. That was the way it was done in traditional Hispanic homes.

My parents were unique partners within traditional parameters, but I didn't feel my marriage gave me a partner so much as it gave me a different home and one that wasn't my own. There was little balance in our relationship. I had no voice in how things were done. Having a daughter made me want a place where my voice, and hers, would always be heard.

I had never lived on my own before, so leaving Richard and raising Arielle as a single, unemployed mother was scary, but not as scary as staying. *Pase, set, remate.*

Fortunately, my brother-in-law helped me land a job for a construction supply company where I learned how to be a responsible adult and parent. Not that I had any other choice.

After divorcing Arielle's father, my mom and I went through a long period where we couldn't seem to relate to each other. She had been with my father since she was twelve years old. The idea that a Caldentey woman would ever leave her husband, or raise a child alone, was utterly alien to her. Her upbringing left her not so much unsympathetic as uncomprehending of my choices. Though she knew unhappy couples, my dad's parents included, and couples that divorced, she never thought these kinds of misfortunes would hit her own family.

She raised me to be an independent, American woman. Yet, in certain ways, she couldn't relate to her American daughter because of her grounding in traditional Cuban and Catholic values. We butted heads a lot in those years, especially during my thirties, when she questioned all of my choices and found them wanting in one way or another. I understood why she felt the way she did. I had listened to the stories, the family history, and absorbed the lessons, but that didn't relieve me of the responsibility of making my own choices, even my own mistakes.

One choice in particular that no one in my family seemed to understand at the time was my choice not to date. I had no intention of trading Richard in for another father for Arielle or another husband for me. My parents' concern that my life would be lonely and somehow incomplete without a husband was not my concern. I tried to make them see that I was okay alone, that I was doing just fine by Arielle, but I don't believe they were ever convinced. Eventually, my brother stopped trying to set me up with all his friends, and my family resigned itself to my singlehood.

When Arielle was five years old, I found a great deal on an all-inclusive resort in Ixtapa, Mexico, and we took our first mother-daughter vacation together. Soon after we returned home, I noticed her stools were bloody. I took her to a doctor, who had no idea what was causing it, but the problem continued. I took her to specialists, who sent her to get all kinds of tests, none of which found anything wrong. Meanwhile, her stools remained filled with blood.

One day her disposition changed dramatically, and she grew lethargic. I couldn't get her to do anything. I called an ambulance, which took her to Cesar Chavez Children's Hospital, where she was quarantined in the infectious diseases unit. The doctors there gave her round after round of tests, all of which revealed nothing. Finally, they did an ultrasound, which showed a mass growing on her liver, but no one knew what it was. Doctors tried one antibiotic after another. None of them did a thing.

I spent every day in the hospital beside her, and in the afternoons, my parents would arrive to keep me company and see if there was any change. I would cry into my mother's shoulder as she held me tightly in her arms. When my mother hugged me, I could feel my body fill with energy from hers, and it would give me the strength to make it through another day of Arielle's illness. My daughter was slowly dying, but with a hug from my mother, I could gather my composure, and I could stop crying.

Arielle had lost an incredible amount of weight. She could barely move when a new Hispanic intern arrived at the unit who had worked in South America and recognized her symptoms as *Entamoeba histolytica*, a parasitic infection found in tropical locations with poor sanitation. The condition kills about 55,000 people a year, and had this woman not ended up on that floor, Arielle would have been another casualty. Once she was properly diagnosed and treated with the right antibiotics, she recovered and was released from the hospital. She'd been there an entire month.

My employer had been supportive during the whole ordeal, and even before, as I faced the hurdles single parents regularly deal with. Still, after Arielle's near death, I realized how important it was that my daughter be my number one priority. Life was fragile, and I needed to be a greater presence in her life. So, after a couple of months, I quit my job and started working freelance and part-time gigs. Now I had time for my daughter, but very little money. When the car would get low on gasoline, I never knew if I would have money to fill it when it came empty. There was a gas station I would drive six miles out of my way for because their bank card processing system took a day for purchases to hit the bank. I could use my debit card there, even when there was no money in my account. It's where I often went when I needed groceries. When things got really bad, I'd escape with a game of volleyball.

Like my mother, I was an avid volleyball player, and I always brought Arielle with me. She enjoyed watching the game, and it gave both of us some precious outdoor time together. Soon I was playing in the local rec leagues, which evolved into beach volleyball weekends. Later, when she was old enough to start playing herself, I took a seat in the stands, cheering for my girl as my mother had always wished someone had cheered for her.

Arielle's athletic ability made her a prospect at schools across the country, including many in California, but she had zero interest in attending colleges in her home state. She had six offers on the table, including Hawaii and Ivy League schools, and yet, coincidentally or not, she accepted the one in North Carolina, which presented the greatest challenges in my visiting. Of all the schools she applied to, she chose the only one without a direct flight, requiring multiple stops and considerable expense. Even though I was proud that she was asserting her independence as I raised her to, the feelings of disappointment at her choice lingered. If you're a parent, you know my attempts to keep those feelings at bay failed.

With Arielle gone and my parents living almost three hours away, I found myself reaching out more to connect with old friends through Facebook. I was scrolling through my feed one day when, quite unexpectedly, I saw a picture of Luis Ocon.

I remembered him as the other Latino in the sea of white faces that made up Glendale High School in the 1980s. He wasn't the funniest guy, nor the most popular, but I remember he treated others with respect. Respect was a trait in short supply among the boys I knew. It made me curious about him, but not curious enough. I was too busy letting the more outwardly confident, brash, and ultimately, childish boys pursue me. Had my mother known about Luis back then, she would have insisted I date him. She probably would have sent my father to Luis's house to invite him over for dinner, every single night if necessary, until "Monica and Luis" was a done deal.

Now in my late forties, divorced, and with a soon-to-be-adult child, I looked at Luis's life as he presented it online, and I was intrigued. I knew better than to believe people's lives on Facebook were as good as they looked, but I saw something in his photos and his interests that caught my attention. He reminded me of my father, and I didn't know any other men like my father. He was an outdoorsman. He hunted. He snowboarded. He surfed. He was stylish without pretension, and funny without ever being mean. Believe it or not, I saw all of this in his pictures, and it reminded me of my father. Luis was a man who lived *con gusto*.

We communicated through social media for a few weeks, and then we began emailing each other. When he asked for my phone number a month or so later, I gave it to him. It had been about eight weeks since I hit the first "like" on his picture, a step I somewhat sheepishly took after he sent me a message saying, "It's great to see you here. I hope your life is full of happiness."

During our first phone conversation, his stories reminded me of my own family. We seemed to have become our parents. Or my parents. I couldn't tell, but it all felt so familiar. Our families were the first Latinos in the elementary schools we attended. His family is Panamanian and Nicaraguan, and he identifies predominantly with the Panamanian side. Panamanian culture is very similar to Cuban culture, especially when it comes to the foods we eat and familial expectations. Both of us represent the first generation of our families born in the US, and like many first-generation Latino-Americans, we grew up speaking Spanish at home. Neither of us spoke much English until we began attending elementary school. Then our parents sent each of us off on the first day and said, "Go learn English!"

We talked about that day with each other, and how difficult it was for us to navigate that landscape as children. Glendale was our home, and yet when we started school, we discovered we weren't fully at home in Glendale. At least not yet. We would be.

When Luis described his first day at school, he said getting through it made him feel as if he could navigate his way through anything. I understood what he meant. It was a sink or swim moment, and in hindsight, we saw that our parents had forced

us to start swimming long before we would have considered ourselves ready. That first day of school, a couple of kids taunted Luis
when he didn't understand how to respond to their questions. He
walked away from them, went behind a building, and when no
one was looking, copied something he saw in a movie. He put his
shoulders back, straightened his spine, and gently slapped himself in the face a couple of times with his hands. Then he walked
back toward the playground. Now he could face anything.

We both had our grandmothers in the house with us as children. Our families went to the same restaurants, the same camping spots, and shopped at the same stores, including El Mambi
Mercado Cubano and everybody's Pasadena favorite, Fedco. We
had lived parallel lives just miles apart from one another. High
school, a mere transversal, made us aware of one another but
didn't change our trajectory. Looking back, it's a mystery our
lives didn't intersect sooner. Looking back, it's a miracle they
intersected when they did.

When Luis invited me on a date, I immediately said yes. It was
my first date in years, but within an hour, I knew there would be
another. Within two hours, I was imagining what our lives would
be like together. Within three, I was figuring out how I was going
to introduce him to Arielle, and then my parents.

Luis and I were together for just a couple of months before he
met my parents. It was October 2009, and I had planned a weekend trip to Napa Valley for the four of us. All my life, my father
had maintained a kind of distance with anyone I was interested
in, including my first husband. He was always polite, of course,
but distant. With Luis, it was completely different. From the first
day, it was obvious there was a kind of chemistry between them.
My mother said it was as if they shared the same soul, like they
were brothers or kindred spirits. They bonded over books, music,

Spanish poetry, world history, and a passion for hunting and fishing. I loved watching them together, as did my mom. We might be walking from our hotel to a restaurant or visiting one of Napa's famous wineries, and my father and Luis would stroll off together, leaving my mother and me to catch up. One evening I noticed that when my mother and I would join them, they kept sharing sly, conspiratorial glances often followed by laughter.

Finally, I couldn't help myself. "What are you two talking about?" I asked.

My father looked at Luis, turned to me, and said, "I'm not sure I can tell you, Monica."

Luis smiled and looked down at his feet before raising his eyes to mine.

"What?" I said with mocking incredulity. "Come on, tell me."

"We're discussing a poem," said my father.

"Oh, really?"

"Yes," he said. "A poem by Neruda."

"Why can't you tell me that? I know who Neruda is."

Luis chuckled at this point, and I could see my father stifle a laugh.

"The poem is called 'Lone Gentleman,'" my father said.

"It's a little risqué," Luis added.

"Really?" I said. At this point, I wasn't sure if I was being teased, or they were serious.

"Yes," my father said.

"Well, what about this poem is so interesting to you two?"

"We're comparing our favorite parts," my father said, and they both burst out laughing.

Until that day, I had no idea Luis knew so much about poetry. I'd never met any man who appreciated and knew something about poetry, especially Spanish poetry, except my father. I never shared his deep appreciation of the art, but I always loved and admired his passion for it. I loved discovering that Luis shared this passion with my father. I loved that he had never felt the need to flaunt his knowledge to impress me. I loved that this man I knew so well had layers yet to show me. I had loved Luis deeply before, but watching him with my father, I loved him even more.

At our last meal of the trip, my father raised his wine glass in a toast and began:

*Despierta. El día te llama*
*a tu vida: tu deber.*
*Y nada más que a vivir.*

These were the opening lines of one of his favorite poems by Pedro Salinas, "Despierta. El día te llama."

*Wake up. Day calls you*
*to your life: your duty.*
*And to live, you need nothing more.*

Luis raised one eye, smiled, paused briefly, then said, "Give me a moment, Armando. Please?"

My father looked at him and nodded. What happened next came as a complete surprise to my mother and me and perhaps sealed my father's affection for Luis Ocon, the man who would become my husband.

With a gentle smile evident in his lips and in his eyes, Luis continued:

*Tu tarea*
*es llevar la vida en alto,*
*jugar con ella, lanzarla*
*como una voz a las nubes,*
*a que recoja las luces*

*que se nos marcharon ya.*
*Ese es tu sino: vivirte.*
*No hagas nada.*
*Tu obra eres tú, nada más.*

*Your work*
*is to lift life high,*
*play with her, hurl her*
*like a voice to the clouds,*
*so she can bring back the light*
*that has already left us.*
*That is your fate: to live.*
*Do nothing.*
*Your work is you, nothing more.*

Poetry was how my father marked a special moment or experience. Seeing Luis celebrate our last night of that first weekend in the same way, surely warmed his heart as it did mine and my mother's. I had never felt so happy as I did that night. How could we have known that eight years later and just a few miles away, we would live out those fateful lines of Salinas's poem during our ninth and final family weekend, hurling our lives against clouds of smoke as we struggled to bring back a light before it left us forever?

# Las Familias Familiares

MY MOTHER'S YOUNGER BROTHER, JUAN, LOVES TO TELL about the time he and his wife Andrea were on a Scandinavian cruise with my parents, and they disembarked for a three-hour stop in Copenhagen, just enough time to do some quick shopping or have a drink onshore. My mother suggested they see Tivoli Gardens; she had read about it in a novel and said it sounded delightful.

"How far away is it?" Andrea asked.

"Oh, it's very close by," my mother said. "We can walk it easily."

Juan wanted to know what there was to do there. He had never heard of Tivoli Gardens.

"Oh, it's beautiful," my mother said. She beamed with anticipation. "And it has to be seen to be believed. It's the world's second-oldest amusement park."

Before my aunt and uncle could argue, my father grinned. "You two know how this is going to end. We might as well get going."

They knew my father was right. Once Carmen set her mind on something, she saw it through. Hadn't she qualified for Cuba's Olympic volleyball team? Hadn't she married my father? Hadn't she chosen to settle her family in Glendale because it sounded like a lovely place?

Over an hour later, they arrived at the gate of Tivoli Gardens. They had walked nearly three miles.

"Oh, my God. Look at the price to get in," Andrea said. A single admission ticket was more than $100 US.

Juan suggested they turn back. "We have about ninety minutes before the ship departs. We don't really have time to see anything here but go in, look around, turn around, and leave. And if we do that, we'll need to take a cab back to the dock."

My mother was determined. "But we're here. We may never have another chance to see it. We have to go in, and if we only stay for half an hour, we can still walk back."

So they bought their tickets, caught a brief glimpse of Tivoli Gardens' legendary magical fairy garden, bought iced tea, and walked back to the dock via a different route because, as my uncle Juan tells it, "Carmen said it would allow them to 'see more of the city.'"

The entire excursion cost them close to five hundred dollars, and they were in Tivoli Gardens for about fifteen minutes.

My father, aunt and uncle laughed about the absurdity of the Tivoli Gardens trip long after they reboarded their ship and set off for Stockholm. My uncle still jokes to this day: "Tivoli Gardens is the loveliest place in the world to have tea. As long as you don't mind it iced. And in a plastic cup. For $125 a cup. That does come with a cookie. One cookie. You might have read about Tivoli Gardens in books, but books don't do it justice. You have to experience it in person."

The humor with which my uncle told the story of The Walk to Tivoli Gardens, as it came to be known, shows how much our family admired my mother's bright and adventurous spirit. She was determined not to waste opportunities to see everything and to experience everything one could experience, and I wanted to have similar experiences with her. I didn't have the time nor the means for trips to exotic locations, but I wanted those more family experiences with them. Arielle was in college, building a life of her own. Luis and I had been together for about a year. We were looking forward to the rest of our life together, and I wanted my parents to be a part of that.

My parents lived in Southern California, hundreds of miles from Salinas, where I lived with Luis, whom they had yet to meet. They had always traveled. Being able to fly for free was one of my mother's favorite perks about her job at United. Now, in retirement, they took cruises to Europe, Scandinavia, and even Russia. They went on hunting and fishing trips to South America and visited Alaska and Japan. Luis and I couldn't join them on these international adventures, but I could do something to share this part of their life with them. We would have to travel hours to visit each other anyway, so why not plan a visit that would be an experience for all of us? Luis shared my parents' appetite for adventure and discovery, and a weekend trip together would be the best way to introduce them to the man who would become my husband. I came up with a list of nearby places Luis and I wanted to visit, or revisit, and called my mom to see what she thought of my idea.

It turned out there were several places in Central and Northern California she and my dad had always wanted to see but never did because their default was to get on a plane or a ship.

"So, you think this is something he would enjoy?" I asked.

"I do, but let me ask him. He's out right now, but we'll talk about it tonight, and I'll let you know. I'll call you tomorrow."

I ended the call with my mom, excited about the possibility of taking a trip with her and Papá and finally introducing them to Luis. It was good to know we'd be creating a different traveling experience for them—one that didn't involve an expensive ticket and jet lag. I would have loved to call my father immediately to tell him my plan, but he didn't own a cell phone. They didn't need two phones, he said, because they were nearly always together.

OUR FIRST TRIP WAS TO NAPA VALLEY, WHERE WATCHING my father and Luis together was like watching Humphrey Bogart and Claude Rains at the end of *Casablanca*. It was also the trip where Luis, entirely by accident, suggested we visit Rafanelli Winery in neighboring Sonoma. How could he have known Rafanelli was one of my father's favorite wines of all time and that my parents ordered it whenever they saw it in a restaurant?

From that year forward, we made an annual trip to a new location. They were always somewhere within a few hours' drive, and we never did anything extravagant. The point was to create simple but memorable getaways with my parents. For my mother and me, these times became a rite of increasing joy between us and led to other trips just the two of us shared. Before the 2015 trip, she and I went glamping at Rincon parkway, and she told me she was having a hard time finding people to play Scrabble with because, after all, she was that good. That's when we discovered Words With Friends. We played this game together for years, texting a running dialogue of commentary on each other's words in the form of kudos or curses.

We usually took our trips together on Mother's Day weekend, but as 2017 approached, we had to push it back a few times because my parents had one engagement after another on their calendars. We finally found a date in October that worked for all of us, which we figured would be the perfect time to visit the wine country. Hopefully, we could capture some Indian summer weather before winter settled in. This trip was extra special because we were returning to the area we took our first trip together in 2009. Also, Arielle would be joining us with her boyfriend, Dennis. I was excited to make this weekend a sextet of three generations.

Once it was decided we would be visiting Napa Valley the first weekend of October, Luis offered to arrange where we would stay. He told me he had something special in mind but assured me he wasn't going to "up the ante." It would still be a low key weekend with no financial or emotional pressure attached. I appreciated his earnestness and happily handed it off to him. My parents were impressed at his willingness to take on the challenge and his ability to keep his plans a secret. My mother would regularly ask me where we were going, and I'd say, "I don't know. Luis has it handled, and he won't tell me. He says we'll find out when we get there, and he promised me we'll like it. End of story, Mamá."

SHORTLY AFTER LUIS AND I WERE MARRIED IN 2014, WE settled in Moss Landing. This small town of fewer than 300 people is twelve miles away from Salinas, nearly equidistant to Santa Cruz at the northern end, and Carmel at the southern. It was ideally situated for Luis to take advantage of everything that mattered to him: surfing and fishing, and I loved its sense of community, something I hadn't felt since living in Glendale in the seventies. Neighbor children play in the street, and on Wednesdays, adults stop to talk to one another as they take their trash to the curb. I love that occasionally someone will knock on our door and ask for an egg, some sugar or flour, or some vegetable oil for a spur of the moment recipe. My parents still lived hundreds of miles away in Southern California, and Luis and I hoped to entice them to settle closer to us.

Friday, October 6, 2017, the day before we were scheduled to drive up to Sonoma, we held a block party at our home. Ostensibly, it was to celebrate the end of a long remodel, but the real reason for the party was to introduce my parents to the neighborhood and tempt them into moving from their home in Apple Valley. Later that night, after everyone had gone home, the four of us sat at the dining table talking. It was too late for games, but none of us were quite ready to go to bed. I took the time to ratchet up my campaign to get my parents out to Moss Landing.

"What did you think of the neighbors?" I asked.

"I enjoyed them," my mother said.

I nodded. "Yes, they're great, aren't they?" My father nodded. "What do you think of the neighborhood? Papá, don't you love how close it is to the ocean?" As long as I could remember, whenever anyone asked him if there was anything in particular he missed about Cuba, he told them he missed living close enough to the ocean that he could smell it.

"I do."

"Can you smell the ocean? That's one of the things Luis and I love about living in Moss Landing."

"It's nice," he agreed, but that was all he said. I looked at Luis. He gave a subtle shake of the head. *That's enough, Monica,* it said. *The evening has already been a huge success. Don't push it.*


THE NEXT MORNING, SATURDAY, WE GOT IN OUR CARS AND headed north toward Sonoma. My parents would be driving straight to Apple Valley from Sonoma on Monday, so they followed behind us in their Chrysler 300.

A month-and-a-half ago, Luis had broken his silence on where we were staying. He had come creeping into the kitchen one afternoon with a Cheshire cat grin and said, "You will not believe what I just did."

"Hmmm. You're probably wrong about that. The question is, will it make me happy or sad?"

"Happy. Extremely happy. And it's going to make Mamá even happier than you."

"Okay, now I'm intrigued. Hint?"

"On a clear day, you can see forever."

"What?"

"On a Clear Day You Can See Forever."

"Isn't that an ancient musical?"

"Yes."

"Oh my God, you crack me up. Tell me!"

"Dan Brown's house is available the weekend your parents are coming up. I mean, it was available. It's not anymore because . . ." he said this while extending his arms, "we're staying there!"

Dan Brown was a friend and colleague of Luis's from the early days of their respective chiropractic careers. I'd never seen this house, but I had heard plenty about it. It had once been Dan's primary home, but now it was usually rented out for extended periods during the year. When Luis found out it was available for this weekend, he could barely contain his excitement. When I found out, I could barely contain mine. It seemed the perfect retreat to enjoy a weekend with my parents and Arielle and Dennis. Anticipation was high.

Our first stop in Sonoma was the Fremont Diner, where we met our friends Joel and Shannon for lunch. Luis and Joel had met in college and stayed close over the years. Joel and his wife Shannon were some of the first people Luis introduced me to once I'd moved up from Newport Beach nearly a decade ago. They lived in nearby Petaluma, and I was excited to introduce them to my parents. My parents and Joel and Shannon thoroughly enjoyed each others' company, and Luis and I enjoyed having them together. It was a hot afternoon, and we were in no hurry to leave. The mimosas we shared at that small table on the back patio of the restaurant were refreshing in the hot Sonoma sun.

After lunch, we said goodbye to Joel and Shannon, got back in our cars, and continued north toward Santa Rosa where we would be staying.

Luis was the only person who knew exactly where we were going, so he led the way while my father followed.

My mom and I played Words With Friends from the passenger seat of our respective cars. Periodically, I would check the side mirror for their Chrysler 300. I didn't want to lose them.

As we drove, I surveyed the houses that lined the road. There were older, humbler homes built before the area had become a tourist destination. Mixed among the old were newer, larger homes built by people with considerably more money, or at least noticeably grander architectural ambitions. All the houses were separated from each other by old oaks, vineyards, and the foot-hills of the Sonoma Mountains. Even as yellow and brittle as the landscape looked, it was still beautiful.

It should have taken us just under an hour to get there, but about twenty-five minutes into the trip, we joined a line of idling cars inching north on the 101 Interstate. A PG&E maintenance crew had closed one of the road's two lanes to work on what looked like transformers.

I got the first text from my mom less than a minute after we'd stopped. They were right behind us.

"What's the problem?"

"I don't know. Luis says it looks like they're fixing a transformer."

"That's what your father said."

"I'm sure he's right. Shouldn't be long."

"I can't wait to see this house."

"Soon Mamá"

"It's your turn. You're losing."

Back to playing Words With Friends.

Once we got past the PG&E crew, we turned west onto Mark West Spring, a two-lane road that took us past Sutter Hospital, John B. Riebli School, and into the Sonoma hills at the southern end of the Mayacamas Mountains where we would be spending the next two days. The further into the foothills we went, the slower Luis drove, and the more his eyes flicked to the rearview mirror, checking that my parents were right behind us. My parents still had only my mom's cell doing triple-duty as phone, GPS, and Words With Friends, so Luis and I were careful not to drive too fast.

On one of our trips, Papá had mentioned getting his own phone. It wasn't right, he'd said, that he always depended on Mamá, and I'd agreed. "At least you could play Words With Friends with me and Mamá."

Mamá had laughed. "He knows better." But even she'd supported the idea. "Mandi, how many times have you wanted my phone to take a photo, or check Google Maps, or to send a message, and I didn't have it?"

"Rarely."

"Rarely you ask, or rarely I don't have it?"

"Both. Besides, if you don't have yours, someone else has theirs." Then he'd said, "No, you're right, Carmencita. I know it's time. You manage everything, and I should take some of that on. And since everything is over the phone nowadays, I guess that means I need one of my own."

"Great. I'll get you one right now." Mamá had picked up her cell, but Papá had waved her off.

"No. We have had this conversation a million times. I have told you I will get a phone, and I promise I will, but it doesn't need to be today."

That had been two years ago.


WE PASSED DONNER DRIVE, WHICH I THOUGHT WAS A TER-ribly inappropriate name for a mountain street, then made a left onto an even narrower two-lane road, Crystal Drive.

The land to the east of us on the right side of the road rose gently with houses set on the hillside, while on the left of the road to our west, ranch-style houses sprawled over large lots landscaped with trees and grass and an assortment of sheds. Utility cables ran alongside the road, strung on tall wooden poles. Further north, the ranch homes on the left gave way to small ranches with animal pens and corrals. Meanwhile, the houses on the right became harder to spot as they were set further away from the road up curving driveways.

As we climbed up the canyon, fewer homes were visible from the road. On our left, I might see a driveway or a roof hidden among trees. On our right, I saw nothing but the dry grass and trees of the hillside.

"We're almost there!" Luis announced as we approached a hairpin turn in the road, past which I could only see a ridgeline topped with trees. I texted Mamá *We're almost there!* and she replied immediately with her trademark heart emoji.

Luis turned the Audi sharply to the right. Where we had been heading north, now we were pointing south. A low stone wall on our left kept vehicles from plunging off the cliff and onto the houses and farm buildings below. Crystal Drive continued its gentle ascent when Luis brought our car to a stop at a narrow fork in the road. My parents' Chrysler idled behind us.

Crystal Drive disappeared in a curve to the northeast, on our left, and according to a casually placed sign, it would "cease to be a county maintained road." Straight ahead, to the southeast and marked with a "No Outlet" sign, was Crystal Court, our destination. Crystal Court sloped gently upward, and from where we were, we could just barely see two houses ahead of us. They sat behind a cluster of large, mature olive and oak trees. One of them, on the right, had an expansive circular driveway giving them two access points to the street.

"Is one of those Dan's?" I asked breathlessly.

Luis laughed. "Not yet," and he put the Audi back in drive. My dad followed behind us.

We continued up Crystal Court for about a tenth of a mile before reaching the house we would call home for the next two days.

Dan's house was the last one on the right, just past its neighbor with the large circular driveway. A low berm separated the two homes giving the impression that Dan's house sat on its own raised platform. The elevation of the home provided an unobstructed 180-degree view of the entire canyon. There were only two other homes across the street. One with a driveway that emptied between Dan's and the circular driveway next door, and the other was situated directly across from Dan's but built slightly higher on the hill on the east side of Crystal Court. Behind both houses was a shallow gully with the roofs of a handful of homes just visible from the street. The vista was spectacular, but much of the vegetation looked brittle and dry.

Standing in front of Dan's house, I focused on two things: the hillsides on the other side of the canyon, which reminded me of the mountains in Glendale where we grew up, and the swimming pool in the rear corner of the flat backyard. The pool was perched so close to the edge of the canyon it resembled an infinity pool.

The sky above was a brilliant blue, streaked with cirrus clouds in the distance. It was a beautiful Indian summer afternoon.

My parents pulled in behind us. The driveway to Dan's house was more horseshoe-shaped than circular and not especially wide—certainly not wide enough for one car to drive around another. I knew my father and Luis would discuss how to park and in what order, since once Arielle arrived, whatever car she parked behind would not be able to get out without someone moving the car in front of it.

For months, my mother had questioned me about this place. First, it was where are we staying? What does Luis have planned? Since I didn't know either, I couldn't answer her. Once Luis told us we'd be staying at his friend's house in the hills, my mother wanted to know what it looked like. Do you have pictures? No. Do you know what style of house it is? No. Well, what's it like? I don't know Mamá, I've never seen it. Well, has Luis seen it? Yes, he's been up there to visit Dan and Joel. He says it's beautiful. He says you'll love it. Oh, I'm sure I will. I can hardly wait. Finally, we were here, standing together before spectacularly large double doors with sidelites of solid glass running the length of the entrance. We had only gotten as far as the front step, and we were both impressed past our expectations.

My mother always carried herself with an elegance and poise that belied her excitable nature. Even at seventy-five years old, she was as prone to giddy delight. Her every move that Saturday afternoon as we stood before the entrance to Dan's house radiated anticipation. Luis punched the security code into a keypad next to the door, there was a click, and we stepped inside.

What immediately struck me was how open the home was. From the front entrance, I could see clear to the back of the house where floor-to-ceiling windows ran the width of the house. Through the windows, I had a view of the entire canyon. The design was strikingly contemporary, with two matching wings of private quarters flanking a central open living space.

The four of us took off through the house in different directions, scoping it out. I could hear my mother talk excitedly from another room and my father laughing with pleasure at her obvious delight. And it was delightful. Most especially because the house was what my mother had always described as her "dream home": open, contemporary, views from everywhere in the house, and filled with interesting, beautiful objects from around the world. We could not have wished for a lovelier home to spend time together as a family.

Although Dan no longer lived there, he had designed the home in such a way that every piece of furniture and every piece of art seemed to tell a story or bear witness to an adventure he'd had. I admired his ability to decorate the house in such a personal way without it being cluttered or making us feel we didn't belong. A lovely and most personal touch was a photograph of Dan, Joel, and Luis from a trip to Brazil they had taken together. Their smiling faces seemed to say, "Welcome home, everyone. You belong here."

The house was gorgeous, but the view from the backyard was spectacular. Standing on the canyon ridge with the valley stretching for miles beneath me, I was reminded of my childhood home in Glendale. It hadn't been as elegant as Dan's, but it was in the hills with a view of the city. I'd been twelve years old when we moved into that house, and I remembered standing on a ridge, like this one, looking over the city, feeling as if our family lived at the top of the world. A lot had changed since 1976, but I felt all the hope, excitement, and gratitude I'd felt that first day at our Mountain Street house. Good things were ahead.

Luis came up behind me and wrapped his arms around my shoulders, bringing me in tight against his chest.

"Unhappy?" he asked. It was a joke we shared from the first Addams Family movie.

"Very," I replied, "Unhappier than I think I've ever been."

"That makes me a most unhappy man."

Then Luis looked over at my parents, who were holding hands and standing at the edge of the patio, overlooking the canyon, and asked, "Mamá and Papá! Are you happy?"

My father smiled at Luis and said, "Very!"

My mother said, "Luis, this is spectacular. Thank you!"

Luis replied with a smile, walked over to the pool at the far edge of the patio, and stuck his toes in the water. The pool was another beautiful part of the whole. Sharply rectangular, with a jacuzzi set horizontally across the far end, it was surrounded by an ochre-tinged concrete apron, which contrasted well with the sapphire blue tiles lining its perimeter. The teal water sparkled invitingly, and a slight wind made ripples across the surface. Two oaks provided some shade at each end, and, in between, chaise lounges beckoned us to enjoy the warmth.

"So, who wants to go swimming?" Luis asked.

We went inside, unpacked our things, and changed into our swimsuits. I found a bottle of wine, and by the time I brought it outside, everyone else was already in the pool. The water was refreshing, but not cold. Dan had just installed a radiant heating system for the pool, which maintained the water at a perfect 86 degrees.

It was October in Northern California, and though the day had been warm, the air around us began to cool as evening approached. Even the 86-degree water produced by the brand-new radiant heating system couldn't keep us from shivering. The four of us moved to the jacuzzi, where we could enjoy the water, and our wine, without shaking.

My father and Luis began sharing favorite memories from previous weekends. My mother sat close to my father as she always did, and as I sat with Luis, I watched my father and Luis laugh together, and I became acutely aware of the concentric rings of relationships that defined our life together. Dan and Joel had been center to Luis's circle for decades; my parents and Arielle had been center to mine. When Luis and I brought our lives together, we brought our circles together, "his" and "hers" was replaced by "ours." My daughter and my parents became ours. His friends and family became ours. That's what made today so special. It wasn't the mimosas at Fremont Diner or Dan's sumptuous house. It was that today we had brought my parents into a circle we shared with Joel and Shannon and Dan, and when Arielle joined us tomorrow morning, she would join the circle as well.

One of my favorite possessions is a portrait of our French bulldog, Bodhi, painted by our neighbor Nancy Russell who lives directly across the street from us. Sharing the spotlight with Bodhi is Joel and Shannon's dog, Brut, who is from the same litter as our own boy Bodhi. This painting is both a reminder and an example of how many connections shape a family. Luis and I came together, not to become one, but to become multitudes, just as my parents had done on a tiny island in the Caribbean over sixty years ago.

# Sunday, October 8, 2017

Arielle arrived at the house early Sunday morning. We were disappointed to find out her boyfriend Dennis hadn't been able to join us. He had to finish up a couple of school projects that weekend, and between taking care of their dogs and her hectic work schedule, she could only spend the day with us before heading home early the next morning. I gave her a tour of Dan's home, which impressed her as much as it did us, then we sat next to the pool to take in the view and morning light, and make our plans for the day. We decided to spend the first half of the day in and around Bodega Bay, drive to Petaluma for lunch with Joel and Shannon, and finish off with some antiquing. For this day trip, we'd all go together in my car.

Bodega Bay was a small seaside town thirty miles west where Alfred Hitchcock filmed *The Birds*. Luis drove, and my father rode shotgun, while I shared the backseat with my mother and Arielle. I loved these kinds of days with my mother because they brought out what I thought of as one of her most uniquely endearing qualities: she was a discerning woman who nevertheless was easy to please. It was her habit to identify and acknowledge the positive and beautiful in nearly every setting and situation. We could take her to a castle, a museum, an amusement park, or a dive bar, and my mom would find joy in each experience. She could savor a moment on its terms without letting anything outside the experience shape her response. The trip to Tivoli Gardens being one example. To my mother, the cost of a ticket, the cost of the tea, the amount of time spent there, and the long walk back had no bearing on her ability to utterly enjoy the fifteen minutes she toured the world's second-oldest amusement park. This ability of hers to appreciate life on its terms was something I did not come by naturally. Still, through decades of watching how she navigated so many diverse circumstances with grace and laughter, I learned to take things in stride and appreciate the unexpected and unusual.

On rare occasions, my father could be critical, but one would never know it in real-time. It was only after the fact, when a person, place, or thing was revisited in some way, that my father might quietly and politely signal his displeasure and then only in terms framed within a general expression of disinterest. If I suggested we return to a restaurant we had once visited, and if he said something like, "Today I think I'd prefer to go to . . ." that would be my first indication he hadn't enjoyed the restaurant on our first visit. Only if pressed directly would he acknowledge his dissatisfaction, which he would still deliver in the kindest of terms. I can't recall a single time when either of my parents used derogatory language to describe a person or place. They loved experiencing life and believed that even if everything surrounding the moment was unpleasant, the moment itself could still provide satisfaction in some way. Whether this was a quality they shared before they met, one they developed from years of being kept apart as teenagers, or cultivated in each other after marriage, I don't know, but it was a quality that made being with them a true pleasure.

As we walked around Bodega Bay that morning, we ended up talking about movies almost as much as we did about the town's beautiful setting. Arielle and I were amused by my mom's excitement to be walking around what was essentially a movie set for Hitchcock's 1963 film.

"Mandi, do you remember when we saw *The Birds*? Wasn't it at the Alex?"

The Alex Theatre in Glendale was an old movie palace, originally built in 1925 as a vaudeville house, and for decades it was the nicest movie theater in Glendale.

"I really don't remember," my father said. He remembered a lot of details, but I knew this wasn't the sort of thing he would keep in his head all these years later.

Turning back to Arielle and me, my mother said, "I think we saw it at the Alex. We loved Glendale. When we first moved there, it felt like we had found the perfect spot in the world to start our life together. Do you remember all the movies we took you to see at the Alex? And how you always insisted on sitting in the balcony?"

"The balcony had the best view!"

"It was more atmospheric on the main floor. I liked feeling like we were in the center of things, not looking down on them," my mother said in her I-know-better tone.

"I still like the balcony," I said.

Arielle chimed in with, "I love sitting in a balcony!"

"Remind me, how are we related?" her grandmother replied, smiling at her.

"Stop," I said, leaning my shoulder into hers.

"Anyway, Glendale was like a big little city. It had nearly everything you wanted without having to drive into downtown or to Beverly Hills or anything like that. It was perfect for us because it was on a scale that was manageable but exciting. We got to know people easily, but it wasn't like Cuba, where everyone was in everyone else's business all the time."

Now she turned directly to Arielle. "This might surprise you, but we tried a lot of different things when we were young. Your grandfather was always looking for opportunities to get ahead, and he had us doing all kinds of things. We bought an apartment building—your Tío Juanin and Aunt Andrea helped us paint it! Juanin was so precise about getting the paint just right I had to yell at him a little bit. I said, "Juanin! Just put the paint on! We need to rent it, not perfect it!"

"Oh my God, I can totally see this! It was the same thing when Dennis and I painted our apartment, but I was Juanin! Dennis kept nudging me the whole time, saying, 'Let's go! Let's go!'"

"We also sold tropical fish."

"No way," Arielle said.

I put my hand over my mouth to cover my smile. I'd heard this one before.

"Yes, your grandfather came home one day and said, 'I have something exciting to show you, Carmencita.' So, he leads me out into the driveway and opens up the trunk of our Impala.

"Inside, arranged on top of blankets, were nearly a dozen little fishbowls, with two fish in each of them. He looked at me with a big smile on his face and said, 'We're going to make a lot of money with these!'

"I said, 'What are you talking about? What is this?' He said these were exotic fish, and people paid big money for them, and we were going to breed them. Then he took me by the hand and led me to the Impala's backseat, where he had all these supplies to set up a tropical fish aquarium. 'Look! It's going to be great.'

"So, he sets up this very elaborate aquarium in the house, where all these fish can breed. And you know what happens?"

"What happens?" asked Arielle.

"Nearly all the fish die within a couple of days."

"Why?"

"A host of reasons, but most of all, your father trusted this guy at the aquarium store who didn't know what he was talking about, and the fish started eating each other!"

Arielle started chuckling. I smiled broadly. My favorite part was still to come.

"Tell her what happened next, Mamá."

"So, almost all the fish die, and some are just floating on the top of the water, kind of eaten up by the others, and I say 'Mandi, this is disgusting. What are you going to do about this?'"

"He says, 'Don't worry, I have a plan.' Plan? Plan for what? A fish funeral business?

"So, I leave it alone, and the next day I come home, and all the fish are gone, but the water is still in the tank. I don't say anything, because I know he feels badly about this little misadventure, and I wait for him to get rid of the tank. Two days later, I came home from work, and the aquarium is filled with goldfish. Different types of goldfish, all swimming around. I said, 'Mandi, more fish?'

"He says he'll do better with these. He had a plan to sell them. And he did. He sold all of them to a coworker of his who was going to use them at some kind of fundraiser. So, I asked him how much he made off this deal."

"How much?" Arielle asked.

"Three dollars and fifty cents."

Arielle started busting up.

"Yes, three dollars and fifty cents, which could buy a couple of hamburgers in those days, but it wasn't a lot of money. So, I said, 'Great. You made a profit. Are we out of the fish business now?'"

I nudged Arielle gently.

"He said, 'No, we need to scale up,'" said my mother, and burst out laughing.

It took Arielle a moment to register the pun, but then she smiled and groaned appropriately. My mother loved a good pun, and fish tales.

After having lunch with Joel and Shannon, we strolled around downtown Petaluma, going into every antique shop we could find. By mid-afternoon, we drove back to Dan's house. I took a brief nap, Arielle talked with her grandparents out by the pool, and Luis began preparations for dinner.

LUIS AND MY FATHER SHARE MANY SIMILARITIES, BUT LUIS is also like my mother in his appreciation of food. His ability to discuss flavors with impressive specificity and precision extends far beyond anyone I had ever seen except my mother.

The four of us would be sharing a meal, and my mom and Luis would have the following conversation:

"What do you think of the amount of cumin they used in this?"

"It obscures the ginger more than I like."

"This really needs fleur de sel."

"I love the way the chocolate has a bit of smoke, but I can still taste the fruit."

"Ummm, bacon?"

They would argue about the source of foods and spend entire evenings discussing the proper seasoning for black beans and how best to prepare rice. My mother and Luis delighted in this epicurean banter, which developed into a kind of routine my father and I found entertaining but largely incomprehensible. Our contributions to the conversation would be to mark the point where one of us would interject and ask the other for some hot sauce or

A1, the mention of which brought sharp frowns of disapproval from our spouses and a shared smile between my father and me.

Of course, one of the benefits of being married to someone with such a discerning palate is being on the receiving end of the food he cooks. That evening, Luis made a fabulous meal of grilled tri-tip and vegetables with an olallieberry pie served with vanilla custard and a glass of cognac. My mother, while a foodie, was also a news junkie. After dinner, she tried to watch some local news and was disappointed to find no cable television in the house. What she found instead was a stash of board games in the same armoire as the television.

She brought out Sorry! and set it up. "Who's next?" she asked with her characteristically broad smile.

Luis raised his hand and said: "I'm in." Arielle did the same. My father was reading something on his iPad and said, "Not me."

"One game before bed," I said.

"Ha!" replied my father.

After a couple of rounds of Sorry! we called it quits. My mother had won both games, playing mercilessly. Once she was assured of victory, she liked to call us her "beloved victims."

At 9:45 p.m., my father and Luis were ready to turn in and let my mother, my daughter, and I enjoy the best part of the night: a fiercely competitive game of Scrabble. After one game, mom and I went to bed and left Arielle to enjoy the rest of the wine, the night sky, and her solitude.

We had no idea what was heading our way, seven miles from us as the crow flies.

**9:22 p.m.**

Eight miles south of 5610 Crystal Court, at 9:22 p.m., a vegetation fire is reported at 310 Buckingham Drive, where Highway 12 meets the 101 Interstate. At 9:23 p.m., eight miles to the north of Buckingham Drive and a mere eight-minute drive from Crystal Court, someone calls to report an "electrical situation" at Maverick Court and Winding View Trail just off Mark West Springs Road. A minute later and five miles to the west, a possible transformer explosion is reported at Fulton Road and Old Redwood Highway, east of Interstate 101. Just over a mile to the west on the other side of the Interstate, a structure is reported burning next to the Hilton Garden Inn.

At 9:30 p.m. and ten miles to the south, a house fire is reported at 203 Orange St. in Santa Rosa.

At 9:32 p.m., there is a report of wires down and a blown transformer on Mark West Station Road.

At 9:33 p.m., a building is burning on North Street.

At 9:34 p.m., a vegetation fire is reported at Primrose Avenue and Todd Road in Rincon Valley, thirteen miles to the south. Fire is also reported at the Silverado Country Club forty miles to the east.

At 9:46 p.m., twenty-seven miles to the northwest of the Silverado Country Club and fourteen miles to the northeast of Crystal Court at Highway 128 and Tubbs Lane near Calistoga, a vegetation fire is reported. The flames spread north, west and south, into the surrounding hills.

**10:00 p.m.**

Ever since she was a teenager, Arielle stayed up later than everyone else, so I wasn't at all surprised when she wasn't interested in turning in with the rest of us.

My mother hugged her granddaughter tightly, *"Hasta mañana, Arielle."*

"Goodnight, everyone," she said. "See you in the morning. I'll be in the jacuzzi with a glass of wine."

I was reluctant to leave her at the pool, but I was tired and ready for bed. I didn't blame her for wanting to stay up longer. Even if Dennis couldn't be here with her, it was no reason not to enjoy the beautiful pool, the solitude, and the views of the hills in the moonlight. Before I went to bed, I peeked my head outside to check on her one last time. It was getting colder outside, and the wind was blowing hard enough that I could hear it from inside the house. Arielle was in the jacuzzi, and she looked so content, I let her be.

I washed up, brushed my teeth, and had finally gotten in bed with Luis when I noticed the wind had picked up even more. From inside our room, I could hear the chairs outside scraping against the concrete patio. Luis lay next to me, his head propped up on the pillows, reading a book.

"Luis, Arielle is still outside in the jacuzzi."

He didn't respond.

"Do you think she should come inside? It's awfully windy outside."

"Sure," he said. "It's cold, it's late, and she needs to leave early tomorrow." Then he turned to look at me. "But who's going to be the one to tell her to come in? You? Me? You know as well as I do how that's going to go."

I knew. Arielle considered herself a kind of Cuban Viking. In college, she had spent many evenings conditioning for volleyball by swimming in cold pools until she was so warmed up she barely felt the water's temperature. It wouldn't surprise me if she sat out there enjoying her wine and the wind for another hour, alternating between the pool and jacuzzi. She was having her moment, in her element, and would not give that up easily. She was a Caldentey woman to the bone.

It was 10:30, just twenty minutes later, when I heard her come in and could finally close my eyes.

## 10:34 p.m.

Between 10:31 and 10:52 p.m., emergency dispatchers are inundated with calls reporting downed power lines, electrical arcing, and fires, most within a twenty-mile radius of 5610 Crystal Court. Sixteen miles to the northwest fire breaks out near Healdsburg High School. Eleven miles away at Oak Leaf Drive and Old Oak Lane, someone reports a blown transformer. Seven miles to the southwest, Monroe Elementary School catches fire, and seven miles to the northeast, on the other side of the valley, firefighters issue mandatory evacuations for all residents.

Sometime around 11:00 p.m., the Tubbs fire claims its first victim.

Michael Dornbach, age 57, is staying with family on Mountain Home Ranch Road, scouting land to build a cabin. As flames approach the house, Dornbach tells his nephew he won't evacuate until he finds the keys to his new truck. His body is found in the driveway the next day.

The town of Calistoga is ordered to evacuate at 11:08 p.m.

At 11:58 p.m., a mandatory evacuation is announced for everyone between the towns of Calistoga and Santa Rosa.

# Monday, October 9, 2017

I WAS DREAMING I STOOD IN A GARDEN OF WILDLY ORNATE orchids sprouting from Byzantine vines, surrounded by lavender bushes and lemon trees. It smelled fantastic. I was turning in circles to take it all in, like a slow dervish. Then Luis was standing next to me, dressed in a cream-colored three-piece suit from the 1920s, with a tan bowler on his head which matched his shoes and reading a timetable for trains. It was as if he had stepped out of an Edith Wharton novel. I turned to him and asked, "Where is the smoke coming from?"

Dream Luis took out his pocket watch, looked at it, and said, "I can't tell. But it's close by."

That's when reality intruded, and I awoke. I looked at the clock. It was 12:25 in the morning. From where I lay, I could see out the window into the backyard. It was even light enough outside for me to see the ridgeline across the valley. "Must be a full moon," I thought. I breathed in and smelled smoke.

Luis had his back to me. He was still. "Are you awake?" I asked.

"M-hmm." He paused for a second, then said, "I just shut the light a minute ago."

"I smell smoke."

"Hmm." Another pause, then, "Yeah. Okay, I do too."

We sat up at the same time. He said, "You check inside. I'll check outside."

"Okay—Wait!" From where I sat on the bed, I suddenly understood why I could see the ridgeline across the valley. "Look!" I pointed out the windows.

The sky just above the ridge was glowing with a faint, orange-yellow haze. "There's a fire somewhere out there."

"Looks far away," Luis said.

"You think there's any danger?"

"I don't know. Let's check the house and the yard, then look online."

Luis went to the backyard, and I headed for the kitchen. I put my hands over the burners. They were cold. I opened the oven and stuck my hand in. It was cold. I stopped and held my breath, listening for the beep of a smoke detector, but I only heard the wind.

I couldn't understand how we could smell smoke so clearly even though the fire looked so far away, or why the air smelled threatening, but I could see no threat. Through the floor to ceiling windows facing the backyard, I saw Luis walking back to the house. He had a troubled look on his face, and a touch of fear grazed the back of my neck. I remember thinking I should close all the windows to keep it from smelling like smoke when everyone woke up and to prevent the scent from seeping into Dan's beautiful rugs and furnishings.

I walked toward the sliding glass door to greet Luis as he came back into the house. That's when I saw what looked like fireflies floating over the patio. I had only ever seen fireflies during trips to Mexico, and I wondered what they were doing here in California. Then I remembered I had just been in the kitchen and had my hands on the burners and in the oven. I looked down at my hands to make sure there was nothing on them I might inadvertently transfer to Dan's furnishings. When I looked up again, the fireflies were still there, and I realized my error. I wasn't seeing fireflies. Those were embers. One hit the glass door at eye level, and I watched another as it drifted slowly to the ground and settled onto the dry grass ten feet from the house. It burst into flames which sputtered across the ground at incredible speed.

Then, as if on cue, a wave of embers rose from the valley below the house, flying horizontally toward it, thousands of them it seemed, and smashed into the sliding glass door. Suddenly, the backyard was on fire, and my husband broke into a run toward the house.

"Fire!" I screamed as Luis flung open the door. He gasped: "We've got a fire. We need to put it out, find a shovel, something!" We dashed to the bedroom. Luis yanked on a pair of jeans and jammed his feet into his shoes. By now, flames were whipping against the house.

Luis took in the situation and changed course. "No, never mind that now. It's too late." He grabbed his phone, wallet, briefcase, and keys and threw them onto the bed. "Get Arielle and your parents. I've gotta call Dan and let him know. I'll meet you at the car. Go."

"Got it," I said, and threw on my clothes from the night before: jeans, a light blouse, and moccasins. I grabbed my phone and ran down the hallway toward the other side of the house where my parents slept.

I banged on the door of their room.

"Papá? Mamá! You gotta wake up! There's a fire, and we need to get out!"

The second of silence that greeted me was way too long.

Finally, I heard my mother's voice through the door. "Monica? What's wrong?"

"Mamá, there's a fire. We've gotta go. Get dressed and meet us at the car. Quickly."

Then I heard my father say, "What's wrong, Carmen?"

"Mamá, now! Tell Papá we have to go now. I have to get Arielle. Now, Mamá!"

I ran to Arielle's room, threw the door open, and yelled, "Fire! Get up, Arielle! We gotta get out of here! Get up!"

She didn't respond, so I ran over to the bed and wrapped her in my arms. She didn't have any clothes on. "Come on, baby. There's a fire! We gotta go! Find something to wear. We need to leave now. Do you understand?" I tried to keep the fear out of my voice, but I didn't feel I was succeeding.

Arielle, perhaps still a little woozy from the wine, nodded and sat up. "Yeah. Okay. Oh, my God. Oh, my God. Yes. I'm moving." I bolted from the room and headed toward the front door and looked outside. The air was smokey, but I didn't see any flames in front of the house. Behind me, I heard Luis calling out to my parents and my mother saying, "We're coming!"

Arielle ran up behind me, wrapped in a towel. She had no shoes on her feet, but she was holding her purse. Did I have time to tell her to put on clothes? Did we have time? Was this important? I decided it wasn't. I threw open the front door. "Come on," I shouted at her, "Get in the car and open all the doors!"

All three of our cars were parked one behind the other in the driveway, facing the direction of the street. Our Audi Q7 was in the front, furthest from the house and closest to the street. My parents' Chrysler 300 was parked behind the Audi, and Arielle's Explorer was closest to the front door.

Arielle hurried toward the Audi. I ran ahead of her and opened up the doors on the driver's side; she did the same on the passenger side and then got in the backseat. I circled the front of the car, so I was on the passenger side. I stood on the floor of the cab and looked back at the house over the roof of the car.

No one was coming out of the house.

I pounded my fist on the roof of the car, "Come on, come on, come on!"

Still, no one came out of the house. By this time, I could see flames leaping over the roofline. I pounded my fists against the roof of the car again, "Come on, come on, come on!" It was all I could think to say.

From inside the car, Arielle gasped. "Where are they?"

I turned to her. "They're coming," I promised. "They'll be right here."

The fire had spread from the back to the side yard. A tree next to the house exploded in flames. I watched as a massive wall of black smoke rose from the valley behind the house. Everything around us was burning, and Luis and my parents were still in the house. What in the hell were they doing? I ran back to the house, terrified and angry, and screamed through the open front door: "Come on! We have to go!" Then I ran back to the car.

*We have to get everyone to the cars. We've gotta get down the hill. We don't have time to take anything with us. We just have to go.*

I was standing by the passenger door of the Audi again, with my back to the street, facing the house when I heard the groan of metal from the backyard followed by an explosion that erupted into a fireball towering thirty-foot over the roof of the house. From where I stood, I could see that fire had engulfed the pool's brand-new solar heater.

Behind me, Arielle screamed and curled into a fetal position in the backseat.

Finally, my mother and father came running out of the house. I noticed they both had shoes on, which told me neither of them was panicking. My mom was dressed in the clothes she had worn the night before. Her attention to apparel and elegance had always been a source of pride for me, but at that moment, I was angry at her for taking the time to look her best. My dad, at least, was wearing his pajamas. They stopped at their car, parked just behind mine. They were planning to drive out in the Chrysler rather than get into the Audi with us. "No!" I shouted. "Come with us! Let's go together!"

My father waved his hand, bidding me forward and yelled something I couldn't understand. They got into their car, with my father behind the wheel, and pulled the doors closed. I heard the engine turn over. Arielle sat up in the backseat.

I looked back at the house. Where was Luis?

With a roar that filled the air, a plume of white smoke climbed up from behind the house, raced over the driveway, and surrounded us. I started choking. I could hear nothing but the roar of the air around me.

Suddenly Luis was there. He was running toward me on the passenger side of the Audi. He was shouting something, but I couldn't understand him over the noise. I also didn't understand why he wasn't on the driver's side of the car. Then he stopped at the back passenger door and addressed Arielle. Now I could hear him when he said, "Arielle, where are your keys?"

Arielle didn't respond. She was looking at something behind Luis and me. When I turned to follow her gaze, I saw smoke was still billowing up from the valley behind the house. When I turned back, she had fished her keys out of her purse and handed them to Luis. She didn't say a word, and she never broke her gaze from the smoke rapidly swallowing everything between our cars and the house.

From the time I witnessed the first ember land on the grass and transform into flame until the moment Arielle gave Luis the keys to her car was less than three minutes. Yet as I watched each tenth of a second tick away, I became frantic. The realization that each passing second put our lives in increasing jeopardy was palpable. I felt compelled to flee but helpless to leave unless all five of us left together. So, when I saw Luis take Arielle's keys, turn, and run back to the house, it was like I was watching him choose death over his family, and I felt helpless.

"What are you doing? We have to go!" I screamed after him.

Either he couldn't hear me, or he ignored me because he kept running and disappeared into the house. I stood there. I waited. We've gotta get down the hill. We don't have time to take anything with us. We just have to go.

Behind the Audi, my parents waited in their Chrysler 300.

Luis was still not back, so I called 911 to tell them about the fire. Just then, Luis emerged from the house with his phone and his wallet in his hand. He waved for me to get in the Audi as he ran toward Arielle's Explorer. "Go!" he yelled.

"No, this one!" I screamed, motioning him to come to the Audi.

"Go!" he yelled, waving me on.

I slammed the passenger doors to the Audi closed, ran to the driver's side, and got in. I wanted Luis to lead the way down, but he was in the Explorer behind my parents, and they couldn't go anywhere until I did. After fumbling to plug my phone into the car's console, responding to the 911 operator, figuring out exactly how far I was from the road, and keeping an eye on Arielle in the backseat, I was ready to go. Apprehensively, I pressed the gas. The

Audi moved forward. My parents followed behind me in their Chrysler, and Luis behind them in the Explorer. We were finally leaving the house.

The 911 operator was still on the line and kept repeating "Fire-Medical Dispatch. Can you tell me your situation?"

"We're at 5610 Crystal Court. There's a fire coming up all around us, and we're evacuating in three cars."

"What's on fire, ma'am?"

"Everything!"

"Is the house on fire, or is it just the vegetation?"

"Everything around the house is burning."

"Is anyone still in the house?"

"No. We're driving out in three cars."

"Does anyone need medical attention?"

"No. But the smoke up here is overwhelming."

"Okay. There are several fires in your area. Please evacuate as quickly and safely as you can. The fire department is out there. Call us back if you need a response."

"Seriously?"

"Ma'am, we're taking hundreds of calls right now. The fire department is in the area. Please evacuate as quickly and safely as you can."

The line went dead.

Smoke suddenly closed in around the car, and I couldn't see a thing.

# Luis 12:30 a.m.

Luis understood why Monica wanted everyone to leave in the same car, but as soon as he realized there was no way they could snuff the fire out he had begun working through possible escape options, calculating outcomes of each:

Scenario 1: Everyone leaves in the same car. That would have to be the Audi. If it gets stuck, gets a flat, or breaks down, everyone is trapped. The car with the best chance of getting them out alive, the Explorer, is back at Dan's house, stuck in the driveway behind the Chrysler.

Scenario 2: They take the Audi and the Chrysler. Something happens to one of the cars, or to someone inside one of them, and both cars have to stop, potentially stranding all of them. The Explorer, still the best car for the job, is sitting back at Dan's house.

Scenario 3: They take the Audi, the Chrysler, the Explorer, and caravan down the canyon. Should something happen to any one car or person in any car, three vehicles give them the most options to continue their escape.

Given the risks of driving out of a burning canyon, the third scenario made the most sense to Luis. Monica and Arielle would be in the Audi. Armando and Carmen would follow in their Chrysler, and he would drive Arielle's Explorer. Fortunately, all the cars were facing the street. That would make pulling out much safer than trying to back out in the smoke. It bothered him that the Audi, not the Explorer, would have to be the lead car. He didn't want Monica to have the stress of leading the way, but at least by being the last car, he could make sure they all made it down.

Luis knew he couldn't explain this quickly enough for it to make sense to Monica; he would just need to act.

He could hear Monica getting her parents up. Good. Armando would know what the dangers were. He and Carmen would be out of the house quickly and without panicking. He dialed Dan's number.

Luis felt horrible. This house, which had been such a vital, central part of his friend's life, was about to be destroyed. He gulped hard, looked around the room, took a deep breath, set his shoulders back, and slapped his cheeks gently. He could hear Arielle in her room, "Oh my God. Oh, my God. Oh, my God." That meant she was up. Good. But where were Armando and Carmen? Why hadn't they left their room yet? He ran to their bedroom on the other side of the house. The door was still closed. He pounded, "Armando! Carmen! You've got to get out of here! The house is on fire!" His mother-in-law answered with an immediate, "We're coming!" Luis turned back to the hallway and dialed his friend.

Through the window, he saw Monica and Arielle were already out the front door, rushing toward the Audi. He saw Arielle had her purse with her. Thank God she always kept it next to the bed on vacation; there'd be no searching for the keys to the Explorer. Why was she in a towel, though? And why wasn't she wearing any shoes?

The phone rang four times before Dan answered. Luis could tell by the sound of his voice Dan had been asleep for a while.

"Hullo."

"Dan, it's Luis."

"I know. What's up?"

"There's a fire up here. It's bad."

"Woah. Shit. Really?"

"Yeah, I—."

"Man, no, sorry. I know. I know. Uh, where are you? Where is everyone?"

"We're getting out right now."

Luis watched through the window as Armando and Carmen dashed across the front yard toward the Chrysler and got in the car.

"Dude, you gotta go," Dan said.

"I know. Is there anything you want me to take?"

There was a pause. Finally, Dan said, "No. Get your family out of there. Get out, Luis, and hurry. It's dry up there. That shit's gonna burn like crazy. Go now. Call me when you're down."

"Okay. Sorry. I'm going."

"Go now, Luis. Now. Hurry."

Just before he hung up, Luis heard Dan turn and say to someone else, "Oh my God," then the line went dead.

Now to get the keys to the Explorer from Arielle.

He ran to the hallway and out the front door. Monica was standing by the open passenger door of the Audi. She locked her eyes on him as he approached; she would be expecting him to drive, but there was no time to explain why he would be in the Explorer. He ran to the passenger side of the car. Through the open door, he could see Arielle huddled in the backseat. She was staring out the rear window, transfixed by the smoke billowing up from the valley floor behind them. He yelled into the open door, "Arielle, where are your keys?!"

Without breaking her stare, she reached into her purse, took out the keys, and handed them to him. Clutching the keys tightly in his fist, he dashed back toward the house, trying to ignore Monica's screams over his shoulder. He just needed a minute. One last check to make sure he didn't forget something. He knew he wasn't going to get a second chance.

Think. Think. Think. What else? There had to be one thing he was forgetting. He turned toward the bedroom. There's no coming back, he thought. What am I missing?

He looked at his briefcase lying on the bed, at his phone in his right hand, and his wallet in his left. It was time to go. Everything else he needed, everyone he needed, was already outside. He bolted through the door, leaving the briefcase behind. There was no reason to take it. Whatever came next, he wouldn't need his briefcase to get through it.

Stepping outside the house less than a minute later, the smoke and the heat of the fire had already intensified. Their window for getting down the mountain safely was closing fast. He ran toward the Explorer, waving to Monica to get going. Reaching the door, he flung it open and jumped into the SUV. He turned the key, praying the engine would turn. The motor sprang to life.

*Okay,* he thought. *Let's get out of here.*

# Armando y Carmen 12:25 a.m.

*Across the ridge from 5610 Crystal Court, artist Sharon Robinson, age 79, dies in her home. Lynne Anderson Powell, age 72, misses a turn as she flees her home on Blue Ridge Trail Road and plummets, unseen, off an embankment. Her husband, following in a separate car, doesn't realize what's happened until days later.*

Armando and Carmen had taken a lot of trips with Monica and Luis by now, and one of the things Armando appreciated about traveling with his daughter and son-in-law was they gave him and Carmen some space at the end of the night. He loved them, but at the end of the day, he wanted some time alone with his wife. Alone at last, they used the last part of the evening to go over the day and share their thoughts and impressions of what they saw and did with each other. Then they fell asleep.

He woke an hour later to an insistent banging and knocking that seemed to come from all directions. For a second, he thought he was dreaming that he was getting an MRI. When he heard Carmen ask Monica what was wrong, he realized the knocking and banging were coming from the bedroom door. While he didn't hear every word their daughter yelled through the door, he clearly heard her say "fire." It took him less than a second to understand the implications of hearing the word "fire" in that place, at that time. He sat straight up in the darkness and tried to orient himself.

"What's wrong, Carmen?"

"There's a fire outside, Mandi. We have to go."

Monica was still pounding on the door. "Mamá! Papá! *Vamonos YA!*"

Carmen called out, "We're coming!"

Armando got out of bed. "You get dressed. I need to use the bathroom."

"Hurry, Mandi."

On the other side of the door, Monica yelled, "Meet me in front of the house! We've gotta go! We gotta get out!"

Armando answered her this time. "Okay! We're coming!" This must have reassured her because he heard her run down the hall toward Arielle's room.

In the bathroom, he used the toilet and splashed water on his face. He wasn't in there a minute, but when he came out, Carmen had already dressed, and the smell of smoke was strong. He was fully awake by now and knew there was no time to get dressed. He leaned against the edge of the bed, put on his shoes, and grabbed his keys and wallet from the nightstand.

They stepped into the hall. From where they stood, the living area was only twenty feet away, and Armando could see fifteen-foot flames approaching the house. *They must have come from the canyon*, he thought. *That means there's a good chance the only way out is into the fire.* While he hated leaving in just his pajamas, he was grateful they hadn't wasted another second. He reached back for Carmen's hand, partly out of habit, partly out of fear, and took it in his, pulling her toward him as they ran toward the front door.

"Lord help us," his wife said.

Armando bent his head slightly down, thinking the same thing.

The front door of the house was open, and they ran through it into a hellscape.

He had an urge to slow down and take it all in. Over his right shoulder, he could see flames encircling the yard on the southeast side of the house and the hill behind it. Off to the right, the night sky glowed a sickening orange. He quickly glanced to his left as they dashed toward their car, and saw flames coming up the hill toward Dan's neighbor's house on the west.

*It's all around us.*

Monica waved frantically at them to get into her Audi, but he held on tightly to Carmen's hand and led her to the passenger side of their Chrysler 300; the more cars they had, the better the chances they would get at least one of them down the hill.

He opened the car door for his wife. He'd been opening her door for more than fifty years. As he closed the door, he looked over at his daughter, her face twisted by anguish just fifteen yards away. He wanted to say something reassuring to her, but what was there to say? This was a time to act. He ran to the driver's side of the Chrysler and jumped in, slamming the door behind him. He jammed his keys into the ignition and was reassured when the car's engine engaged.

Carmen said, "This looks very bad. What do we do?"

He replied, "We wait for Luis to come out, then we follow them down the hill. It will be okay."

She said, "Please, God, let us be safe."

Armando kept his left hand on the wheel, his right hand on the gear shift, and his foot on the brake. He kept his eyes focused on the back of Monica's Audi. He wanted to be ready to shift into drive the instant she pulled away. He wondered why Monica had not turned on her car. For a split second, he wondered if he shouldn't turn off the engine to conserve fuel. His eyes flicked to the gauge, well over half a tank, plenty of gas to get them out of the canyon. His eyes flicked back to the windshield, and he felt a flash of panic. White smoke billowed around them, and he could no longer see the Audi's bumper. Had she already pulled away? Then a gust of wind, a dark flash to the left of the Chrysler, and a startled cry from Carmen.

"Mandi, it's Luis! We can go!"

Immediately, Armando shifted into drive, gripped the wheel, and peered through the windshield. Nothing. Seconds ticked by, and he became acutely aware of the groans and explosions from the fire just outside their car. He eased off the brake just enough to move the Chrysler forward a few inches, and there they were, the Audi taillights, glowing a faint red through the smoke. He advanced as close as he dared and followed them down the drive.

# Monica 12:35 a.m.

As I crept down Dan's driveway toward the street, the smoke pressed against the Audi as if to smother us. It wouldn't be the first time that night I would feel like prey, hunted by something diabolically cunning and fixated on my death. It was as if the fire, having failed to murder my family and me in our sleep, had conspired with the smoke to kill us while we tried to drive blindly toward safety. I hit the brake, allowing myself a split-second of panic, then slowly lifted my foot. The car inched forward, and I forced myself to focus on keeping my daughter safe and getting the car on the road. I couldn't see anything through the windows, so I drove by feeling my way along the asphalt underneath us.

Arielle asked, "Is someone coming to help us?"

"You mean 9-11? I don't know, baby. They said we've gotta get down the hill on our own. It'll be okay. Stay calm. Can you see anything?"

"No," she said.

I couldn't either, but I squinted into the smoke anyway.

With nothing to see, I inched forward, driving by feel. Dan's driveway was asphalt. The street was asphalt. But where the driveway met the street, there was a seam. I peered into nothing-ness and inched forward, feeling for the seam. I prepared to turn left, slowly, slowly as soon as I felt the tires hit the seam.

Slowly. Slowly. I inched forward, feeling for the seam. Nothing.

Nothing? Did the asphalt feel different underneath the car? I inched forward. It did. The road felt bumpy and uneven. I slowed. "Can you see Abu?"

Arielle turned and looked out the back window.

"No. Yes. But barely. They're right behind us."

Thank God. I inched forward. The road was still bumpy under-neath the car. "Can you see Luis?"

"No, not at all." Arielle started to cry in the backseat. I knew I needed to stay calm to prevent her—both of us, really—from melting down. I also knew I needed to keep talking, thinking, and think out loud so she would know we were moving forward. She needed to know we would be okay. I had no idea where Luis was, but in the rearview, through the smoke, I could just glimpse my father's Chrysler. Either the smoke had cleared, or he was mere inches behind me. I looked for the road through the windshield. Nothing. He was inches behind us.

I inched the Audi forward, slowly, slowly, feeling for the seam, so I would know when to begin turning the wheel to the left. My father stayed right behind me, but it was getting harder to see his car in the rearview.

I peered back into the smoke. Nothing. Where was the seam? Why did the road beneath the wheels feel so rough? So bumpy? I was moving so slowly the speedometer wasn't even registering our speed, but the car rocked and pitched as I moved forward. This was wrong. I must have driven off the pavement somehow. I inched forward in the smoke. The car pitched to the right. I was definitely off the road. Either I had inadvertently angled the Audi to the left in anticipation of a left turn onto the road and was driving through the front yard of the house with the circular driveway, or I had driven past the seam, across the road and was in the front yard of the house across the street. I couldn't tell.

I inched forward. I didn't care stop. As long as there was ground beneath the wheels, I would keep the car moving. If I was on the next-door neighbor's lawn, I would feel their driveway beneath my tires. A burst of flame revealed a huge tree, burning to my right. Another explosion to my left, and where seconds ago there had been nothing but smoke, I saw a tree engulfed in flames. Branches exploded, sending embers raining over the car. Keep going, I told myself.

"Keep going," I said out loud for Arielle. "Keep going."

I kept going—inch by inch, my foot hovering over the brake. The car continued to list slightly. I was sure there was no pavement underneath the tires. We were engulfed in smoke. I couldn't see through the windshield. I couldn't see if my parents were still behind me. I couldn't see the trees that had been burning a few feet from my car just seconds before. I couldn't see if I was about to drive off the side of the mountain.

I stopped.

Then I heard the horn of the Explorer.

Luis.

# Luis 12:35 a.m.

As soon as the Chrysler began moving down the driveway, Luis followed close behind. The Explorer was sturdy, but its suspension was inferior to the Audi or even his in-laws' Chrysler, and when the SUV began rocking, he immediately knew they had missed the road. He turned the wheel slightly to the right, and within seconds, the ground beneath him leveled out. He was back on the road.

Unfortunately, Monica and her parents weren't. He needed to get them back, but visibility was near zero, and he couldn't risk all three cars by driving the Explorer off the road without knowing what he was driving into. Then the wind whipped just enough to create a gap in the smoke, and he saw the Audi. It was inching toward the neighbor's house, just a few yards from plowing into the east wall. Every tree on the lot was engulfed in flames. Following right behind the Audi was the Chrysler. Both were oblivious to the danger they were driving into.

Luis laid on the horn. The Audi didn't stop. Neither did the Chrysler. He pumped the horn frantically, hoping to catch their attention. Both cars kept moving toward the house. He kept honking, but the roar of the wind driving the fire was so loud he could barely hear the horn himself. He tried flashing the Explorer's headlights, but they just bounced back off a wall of smoke in front of him. Accelerating as much as he dared, he turned into the yard and drove toward his wife's car. Visibility wavered between zero and shadows. Most of the time, he was driving blind. The smoke would clear just enough to see he was still headed toward the Audi, and the Audi was still headed toward the house, then both cars would disappear again in the haze.

Luis was about ten yards away from the Audi when he realized he would be too late. He hadn't stopped honking since he turned into the yard, but it had made no difference. The sound didn't carry through the smoke. He had no way of warning Monica of the danger she was in. The only way to prevent his wife from driving into the wall was to hit the Audi. If he did this right, Monica would slam on the brake, and the Audi would be spared serious damage. If he did this wrong, he could disable both cars, stranding everyone on the mountain to die.

He pleaded with God to let his plan work as he laid on the horn of the Explorer. The windows were down, smoke poured into the car, choking him, but he screamed, praying that somehow Monica or Armando would hear his voice.

At that moment, the wind suddenly, miraculously, shifted. A small break opened in the smoke. Luis saw the Audi. Miraculously, Monica had stopped. Luis gunned the Explorer and pulled up alongside the passenger side of the Audi. He immediately switched his foot to the brake, and frantically motioned for Monica to roll down the window. He checked the rearview mirror for Armando and Carmen and was relieved to see them stopped behind the Audi. Monica rolled down the passenger window, and Luis watched the interior of her car fill with noxious smoke.

"You're not on the road!" he screamed. "Follow me!"

Monica nodded and gave him a thumbs up. He turned the Explorer to the right and headed back to the road. Over his shoulder, he saw Monica take a hard pull to the right on the Audi's steering wheel to get behind him, and in the rearview, he watched Armando do the same as he maneuvered to stay right behind the Audi. Everyone was riding the bumper of the car in front. Luis's hands, which had been clutching the wheel, relaxed slightly. Now they had a plan: he would take the lead, and they would caravan down the canyon and off this burning mountain.

The sense of relief was fleeting. Through the rearview, Luis could see Monica was struggling to maintain the delicate act of following closely enough that she didn't lose him but not so close that she rear-ended him. He was sure her father was having the same struggle behind her. The smoke would shift unpredictably, blindingly. The Audi would be behind him. The wind would shift, and it would disappear. Shift, and the Audi would suddenly reappear. He regularly looked for a sign of the Chrysler headlights, but he could see nothing behind Monica, which made him nervous.

Suddenly, the Explorer began to rock again. He must have drifted off the road. Thank God for that suspension. Luis had no way of knowing if the road was to his right or his left, so rather than just turn the wheel one direction or another, he swerved the Explorer slowly back and forth, feeling for pavement beneath the wheels, peering into the haze for any sign of the road, a yellow line, the shoulder, even a parked car. Having watched his wife and father-in-law nearly drive straight into the wall of a house, he knew it could easily happen to him. Flaming branches fell from the smoke on his left. Embers hit the Explorer's windshield and melted into the glass. *Burning trees on my left mean the road is probably to my right.* Right. Left. Right. He continued his slow, steady swerve while moving gently to the right.

There was a jolt, a lurch, and the Explorer leveled out. He'd found the road.

Inching forward, he caught the reflection of the yellow dividing line in his fog lamps. He maneuvered the Explorer to the center of the road and maintained his position by swerving from one side to the other over the yellow stripe. *Follow the line,* he said to himself. *Follow the line down. Take it slow.* He knew Monica could see the road no better than he could. Years of experience hunting had also taught him a moving target is easier to see. Hopefully, swerving over the line this way, Monica would have an easier job following him. Hopefully, she wouldn't think anything was wrong. *I hope she understands what I'm doing. Monica. Monica. Please don't lose me.* Occasionally he risked a peek in the rearview mirror to see if she was still there. She was.

Flames licked both sides of the SUV, flowing over the windows, tendrils leaping over the hood as if trying to pry it open.

Luis had heard people describe fear as feeling their heart pounding in their chest. He'd thought it was a figure of speech, but sitting behind the wheel of the Explorer, trying to find his way through the smoke, he could literally feel his heart pounding forcefully in his chest as he tried to blink the sweat out of his eyes while driving as fast as he dared down the road. At every slight bend, Luis feared losing sight of the yellow stripe, sending them all crashing down the side of the burning hill. He was also trying to make sure they could keep up with him. Not too fast, not too slow. He could not fail. The lives of the people he loved depended on him finding a way down.

His next glance into the rearview mirror confirmed his worst fears. There was nothing behind him. There were no lights of any kind, just the reflection of the Explorer's taillights on the smoke when he tapped on the brake pedal. He waited a few seconds for his wife's headlights to appear through the haze, but it was useless. There was too much smoke for him to be sure of anything, and if he didn't start moving, she might hit him. He had to have faith; Monica and Arielle were still behind him. He had nothing else to go on. Luis prayed Monica could still see him even though he couldn't see her and that Armando and Carmen were right behind her. He tapped the brakes with each turn of the wheel, hoping she would see the lights and make the turn with him. After he swiveled the SUV back and forth over the yellow line a dozen times without seeing any headlights behind him, he decided he had to trust they could make it down on their own. He could stop and risk the others crashing into him, or he could push slowly ahead. Neither option felt right, so rather than decide one way or the other, he let the Explorer inch forward, hoping to see Monica come back into view.

Embers lashed the Explorer's windshield, burrowing into the glass. Some rained from the trees, but most flew straight at the windshield. Luis knew that embers blow away from a fire, not toward it, which meant they were driving straight into the fire. He gripped the wheel tighter and blinked the tears and smoke from his eyes. He would be ready.

He came to a bend in the road, slowed, and tapped the brakes just in case Monica was behind him. He turned.

Flames raged in every direction. Both sides of the road burned, and a wall of flame blocked the way directly in front of him.

Instinct screamed to hit the brakes and turn to avoid the wall, but there was no avoiding the flames. They raged to the front, to the left, and to the right of the Explorer. He had two choices: he could stay on the mountain and burn to death in his car or drive through the fire on the only road out of the canyon.

He couldn't see through the wall of fire in front of him. He didn't know how deep it was or how bad things were on the other side. He had no way of knowing if he'd be running into some-thing or driving straight off the mountain. He wouldn't be able to see any turn in time to make it, and wouldn't be able to signal Monica behind him to let her know what was coming.

He wanted to shut his eyes, but couldn't bring himself to. He wanted to stop the Explorer, but he didn't. Instead, he kept his foot hovering between the accelerator and the brake pedal, took a deep breath, and let the Explorer roll into the fire. Having made the decision to keep going, part of him wanted to press down on the accelerator and just get through it, but he couldn't risk losing his family behind him. *Steady, and forward*, he said to himself.

Flames swallowed the Explorer, roaring and clawing at it from every side, underneath, and above. Fire raced across the hood of the car, up the windshield and onto the roof. The car shook and groaned as if being attacked, while he gripped the steering wheel as tightly as he could. Through the smell of the smoke came a new, pungent stench. The SUV was burning. What part he didn't know. It could be the tires. It could be everything. He had never felt such heat in his life, and he wasn't sure the steering wheel wasn't melt-ing in his hands. He lifted his hands from the wheel to see if they were blistering, and he saw they weren't. Before he had taken hold of the wheel again, the SUV rolled out of the flames.

He gasped. He could see. He could see the pavement stretch-ing ahead of him. He could see the flaming trees on both sides of the road. He realized he'd been holding his breath and exhaled. *Keep breathing.* His mind quickly registered that while this was better than what he had just driven through, neither he nor his family was safe yet. He glanced behind him, where the wall of fire still burned. Nothing. He pumped the brakes a couple of times, hoping Monica might see the lights and know he was there.

He continued to move slowly down the road. He passed a pickup truck engulfed in flames. It was parked in front of a house he remembered from their drive up that afternoon. There had been chicken coops on the property. He pictured all those chickens burning to death in their coops, and a wave of nausea hit him.

He glanced again in his rearview mirror to see if Monica and Armando were behind him, but all he could see was the wall of fire he had just come through.

"Come on, honey, please," he said, and at that moment, smoke billowed in from somewhere behind him and cut off his view. He pounded the steering wheel in frustration. He pumped his brakes a handful of times, just in case they happened to pass through the fire with the smoke. Just in case they were there.

Above him, he heard a tree explode, followed by raining embers and fiery pieces of bark falling over the road and onto the car. He swerved to avoid a large flaming branch as it crashed to the ground, partly blocking the road. Once he'd got around it, he moved back to the center of the road, hovering over the yellow line, checking and rechecking the rearview, tapping the brakes.

Another explosion, much louder and from across the road, shook the car. A fireball pierced the thick smoke, and in its flaming light, he saw the explosion had come from one of the houses clinging to the side of the hill. *It must have been a propane tank.*

Another flaming branch fell to the ground, missing the SUV by an inch and bringing with it another shower of embers. He forced his mind back to the road. They weren't out of this by a long shot.

# Monica 12:37 a.m.

VISIBILITY HAD BEEN NEAR ZERO SINCE THE WAVE OF white smoke had billowed out of the valley on the south side of Dan's house and washed over the canyon. At first, I had been glad for the wind. It would periodically clear the smoke just enough to see. Now, the smoke was so thick that the wind, when it blew, would make the smoke dance and swirl in a way that diminished visibility to a terrifying degree. Not only was it impossible to see anything in the dancing smoke, but it moved in a way that created shadows of things that weren't there and made me question everything I thought I saw.

Thank God Luis was leading us out of here. With him now in front of us, I was less afraid. He seemed to know exactly where the road was and had no trouble staying on it. I followed his bumper as closely as I dared so that I wouldn't lose his taillights in the smoke. Every time those brake lights on the Explorer would flash, I tensed, knowing a turn was coming, terrified I would lose him and drive us over the embankment.

From the backseat, Arielle said, "Mom!"

"Yes, Arielle?"

"Tell me we're gonna make it down."

"We're gonna make it down. I promise you we're gonna make it down."

"Why are we in separate cars? I'm worried about Abu and Abi."

"Ari, I don't know. I need to follow Luis. Can you watch the sides of the car for me? Tell me if you see anything I need to avoid?"

"Yes. I'll do that. Do you want me up front?"

"No, baby. Stay in the back. Pray for us, and keep your eyes open, okay?"

"Yes."

"Are you okay?"

"I'm scared." It was the first time in her life I had heard those words from her, and I thought she had a right to be.

"I am too, baby, I am too."

Actually, I was terrified. I was terrified of losing Luis. I was terrified of burning to death in the Audi. I was terrified of losing my parents behind me. I was terrified of completely unraveling in front of Arielle.

When the Explorer began weaving slightly, I worried something might have happened to Luis. The interior temperature of the car had risen sharply, and trees were burning on our left. Perhaps he was swerving to avoid danger I couldn't see. Sure enough, he began weaving to the right. *Thank God for you, Luis. If we get out of here, it will be because of you. I love you.*

From the backseat, Arielle said, "Mom, I think the car's on fire. I can feel the heat coming up from under the car and through the doors."

"We're not on fire. Take your feet off the floor."

"What happens if the embers get into the engine?"

"Arielle, please! Stop!"

I didn't know if we were on fire or not. What I knew was that I couldn't think about it. We had a long way to go before we could get out of this car, and I couldn't think about what would happen if the car caught on fire. There was no way we were getting out of this without a car.

A flaming branch dropped on the hood, and I screamed, causing Arielle to do the same. Cutting through all of the other smells of burning, I could distinctly smell rubber. I wondered if the Audi's tires were melting. *Please, God, let this car make it off the mountain in one piece.*

I hadn't seen Luis's taillights in a while, but I figured he must be just ahead of me. If I was still driving, so was he. The smoke looked brighter and danced around more. I wondered why. I slowed as we approached a turn, hugging the right shoulder to keep far from the embankment on our left. The smoke thinned as I brought the Audi out of the turn, and I looked ahead, hoping to see the Explorer. There it was, ten or twenty yards ahead of me, and just ahead of it was a wall of flame that towered and roared over our only way out.

I slowed the car to keep from hitting Luis, who looked as if he'd stopped. I continued inching forward, though, so my parents wouldn't rear-end me. I had closed the distance between my car and the Explorer by half when I realized Luis hadn't stopped. He'd only slowed, and he was driving into the flames. I watched as the fire swallowed him, and then he was gone.

I didn't want to follow him. Couldn't I just stop right here and somehow wait this out? But what about my father and mother behind me? I could see nothing in the rearview mirror but smoke, but they had to be there. I couldn't make that choice for them. I had to follow Luis into the fire.

"Hold on, baby!" I yelled to Arielle, huddled in the center of the backseat.

"You've got this, Mom. Do you hear me? You've got this!"

I heard a determination in her that hadn't been there before, and I used it to move forward. I pressed down on the gas and urged the car into the flames.

Everything became fire and black smoke. My heart leaped maniacally inside my chest as if it were trying to escape through my throat. The temperature of the car spiked, and sweat streamed down my face and arms and hands.

"I can't see anything!" I screamed.

"Just keep going!" Arielle pleaded from behind me.

I felt her hand on my shoulder. She was leaning forward, one hand on me, the other on the shoulder of the empty passenger seat. I had to fight the urge to press down on the accelerator to get through this as quickly as I could, out the other side, knowing if I did, I could rear-end Luis and trap all of us in this inferno.

"You've got it. Keep going, Mom!"

"I still can't see!"

"Keep going!"

Flames washed over and around and under the car. It was like being in one of those car washes where your car moves along a track while water sprays at you from every direction, and you can't see a thing. And instead of water, there was fire. And there was no track. And death, not the sun, waited for us at the end. Arielle took her hand off my shoulder and curled up in a ball on the backseat. I could still hear her voice, but I couldn't make out words. I wasn't sure if she was speaking or moaning. The interior temperature of the Audi spiked even higher. The steering wheel was like scalding plastic in my hands. The sweat from my palms made it hard to hold. I struggled not to let go.

*We're going to die. We're going to be burned alive.*

I began to pray. *Please, God. Get me through this. Let us live. Please, God.*

From the backseat, I heard Arielle, "You've got this mom! Keep going!"

I was sure these were the last words I would ever hear, and I couldn't turn around or look in the rearview mirror for one final look at my daughter.

*The whole world is burning, and we're burning with it.*

I don't completely trust my memory of what it was like to drive through those flames. When I think about it, there's a heightened clarity in my awareness of the danger, mixed with an all-encompassing dread that twisted perception into hallucination. I know I screamed when a tree branch landed on the hood of my car. I know I slammed on the brakes and watched it roll off and land in front of the vehicle. I know I drove straight over it, thinking it would ignite the tank, and I would die with my daughter in the inevitable explosion. There was a sense of detached awareness. Time was something I could feel stretching and compressing around me. Seconds slowed until time seemed to melt. The world became grossly loud, overbearingly hot, and insanely bright as we drove straight into this white-hot sinkhole of molten sludge. I was spinning in one of those carnival barrels where the floor drops out from underneath you while centrifugal force pins your body to the wall.

I remember I started to cry and told Arielle, "We're never gonna make it."

I remember from somewhere in the backseat I heard her say, "We are going to make it! Just drive!"

I remember hearing an explosion and feeling the shockwave buffet the sides of the car.

I remember being sure it was going to push us right off the road.

And then as quickly as we plunged into the flames, we came out the other side. On this side of the flames, the smoke was thinner, and the wind kept blowing it out, enabling me to see what was going on around us. I saw the Explorer just ahead of us on the road, and a burning pickup truck on my right. I hit the brakes, then quickly realized how stupid that was and hit the gas, causing the Audi to lunge forward. I had to turn wide to avoid hitting the pickup truck, vaguely aware it might blow up at any second. For a moment, I thought I was going to lose control of the car, but then I steered it back toward the center of the road, toward my husband in my daughter's car.

The fire was still everywhere on a scale that filled me with equal parts terror and awe. I knew the danger was far from over, but surely we had just gone through the worst of it.

I pulled the Audi right up behind the Explorer and exhaled. I was drenched in sweat, but it was already evaporating in the heat.

"You did it!" Arielle screamed in the backseat. "Oh my God, Mom, you did it."

Then I looked in the rearview mirror and knew the worst was yet to come. My parents weren't behind me.

# Armando y Carmen 12:36 a.m.

*Mike Grabow, age 40, and his six-month-old French bulldog, Stax, die in their home. Earlier in the day, he had been in one of his favorite local bars, handing out hope bracelets he purchased to raise funds for breast cancer research.*

CARS HAD BEEN GOOD TO ARMANDO BERRIZ. HIS FATHER'S car business had provided well for their family in Cuba. Cars had given his family the opportunity and the means to immigrate to America. Armando had worked side-by-side with his father during summers and semester breaks from college to build the business in a new country. Cars had paid his tuition to Villanova. His parents' wedding gift to him and Carmen was the car that took them to Glendale, where they started their life together. Automobiles had played pivotal roles in many of his most memorable and transformative moments, and as a result, Armando loved to sit behind the wheel of a car. Until now.

As he waited behind the wheel of his Chrysler for his daughter to start moving, he kept focused by engaging in his habit of running through possible scenarios, simultaneously estimating the odds of each outcome. None of them looked good to the man whose success in life had a lot to do with his ability to find solutions to problems others couldn't fix.

Finally, the Audi moved forward into the smoke and almost vanished. He tapped the gas a couple of times to get close to the Audi's rear bumper, careful not to hit the car, and staying mindful of his wife next to him in the passenger seat, sitting ramrod straight, staring ahead with terror written across her face. The Audi's taillights created a red glow inside the Chrysler's cabin, and bounced off the smoke outside the car's windows, creating a shimmering effect reminiscent of a carnival funhouse.

He kept right on the Audi's tail, trying to leave only six inches at best between the cars, hovering right behind, his foot suspended above the gas pedal. It was the only way to assure he wouldn't lose the Audi in smoke and become separated from his daughter and granddaughter.

He saw the Audi dip slightly down. To most people, the subtle change of the car's path might not have even registered, but Armando had spent a lifetime observing how things worked, and the Audi's dip carved out a large pit in his stomach. Armando Berriz was no stranger to cars, and he knew immediately they were no longer on the road. He stayed right behind Monica anyway, because he didn't want to let her out of his sight. The smoke was thick. Visibility fluctuated between zero and a few yards. With all the oak and olive trees, mailboxes sitting on posts at the side of the road, telephone and utility poles, posted signage, the risk of either one of them running their car into something increased by an order of magnitude the longer they were behind the wheel. Fortunately, Monica was driving a well-built car, and she was going slowly enough that even if she hit a tree, it was unlikely to cause much damage. Still, he wanted to be ready to load his daughter and granddaughter into the Chrysler if necessary.

The Audi moved slowly, carefully, which reassured him, but he had the sense it was drifting to the left. Consciously trying not to make his concern visible to his wife, he tried to recall if there was anything between them and the hillside that fell to the valley. Where were the trees? Where exactly was the neighboring house? Armando noticed how tightly his hands gripped the steering wheel, and he quickly glanced over at his wife to see if she noticed. She was staring straight ahead, eyes squinting hard, the corners of her mouth pointing down.

"Mandi, I don't like this," she said. For the millionth time during their life together, she could glean what he was feeling without having to look at him. Her ability to read the air between them was a skill that never ceased to amaze him and grew more refined over the years.

"Neither do I."

"I can't see anything. I'm sure Monica can't see anything, either."

"I know."

He kept his eyes on the Audi's taillights, and when they flashed red, he braked gently but immediately. The smoke cleared slightly, and on his right, he saw Luis driving toward them in Arielle's Explorer.

"Oh my God, what's happening?" Carmen asked.

"I don't know. I think he's trying to signal her."

"About what? What's wrong?" she asked urgently.

"I think we've driven off the road."

"*Ayúdanos, Jesús*," she said softly but forcefully.

Luis passed their Chrysler and edged up to the Audi.

"He has it under control," Armando said, referring to Luis but realizing his wife would take it differently. He didn't bother to clarify. Surely God had things under control, too.

"I can't believe this is happening," she replied.

Within seconds, the Explorer turned right and headed back toward the street, and Monica pulled the Audi in behind it, following. *Good.* Armando thought. *Luis has a plan to get us back on the road.* He cranked the steering wheel just a little tighter to leave some room between the cars, and lifted his foot off the brake. This should have put him in position to keep right behind the Audi, but almost immediately, there was a thump, a bang, and the Chrysler came to a complete stop.

"What happened?" Carmen asked.

"I don't know. Hang on."

He pressed down hard on the gas to free the car, but nothing happened. It wouldn't move. He put the vehicle in reverse and floored the gas pedal, hoping the Chrysler would release. The engine revved, but the car didn't budge. They were stuck.

He looked up and saw Monica's Audi disappear into the smoke. He flipped the car back in park.

"What's going on?" his wife asked.

She sounded worried, so he modulated his voice accordingly. "We're caught on something," he replied casually. He hoped he sounded calmer than he felt.

He put the car in reverse again and tried backing out. This time he eased his foot onto the gas, gently, hoping it would facilitate traction. The car edged an inch and then stopped again. He tried forward and back, turning the wheel left and right, forward and reverse half a dozen times. Nothing worked.

"We're stuck on something," he said again.

With a roar, something just ahead of him went up in flames. The smoke cleared, and Armando could see it was a house, four yards in front of his car. *That's the direction Monica and I were driving,* he thought. He gauged the distance and calculated she had been less than five seconds from driving straight into the wall of the house. He'd thought he had the situation under control from behind the wheel of the Chrysler, but the danger was far worse than he'd imagined. The gravity of their situation washed over him. He and Carmen were trapped, and they had no good options. There was no way to formulate a plan, propose an alternative, or come up with a solution no one else had considered. What he needed most was time—time to think of something— and he was acutely aware he had no time. They had no time.

The flames illuminated the scene enough for Armando to recognize they were in Dan's next-door neighbor's front yard. His daughter had mistaken the neighbor's driveway for Crystal Drive. His mind raced as he tried to orient where they were stuck in relation to Dan's house and how the driveway and road led back to it. There were no streetlights, and now it was nearly impossible to see anything through the smoke. He wasn't entirely sure where they were in relation to where they had left; he'd been paying too close attention to following Monica to know precisely where she was driving.

Fire now rained down around them. There was simply no way he could get out of the car, figure out what they were stuck on, and fix it without getting burned. The heat coming through the windows was already stifling, and if they stayed put, it would kill them. They were trapped.

"I can't see Monica or Luis," Carmen said.

Armando looked over to where he had last seen his daughter disappear into the smoke. No Audi. No Explorer. Again, he forced himself to sound calm. "Neither can I. Do you have your phone?"

"It's in the house."

They had no way of alerting Monica or Luis to their situation, and Armando's mouth filled with a new and bitter kind of fear. Why had he put off getting his own phone for so long?

He laid on the Chrysler's horn. If Monica or Luis were still nearby, hopefully it would get their attention. He laid on the horn again, stopped, and listened for one of their horns in reply. All he heard was the roar of the fire and the wind whipping the car about. Carmen was breathing heavily, which worried him.

Armando suspected Monica's car was just beyond his field of vision, maybe not even twenty feet away, and just in front of her would be Luis in Arielle's Explorer. The smoke was too heavy to breathe, and it would be foolish to risk going into it on foot; they'd be lucky to get further than ten steps from the car. Armando knew they could not make it down the mountain on foot. Wherever they were, they were moving away.

"I don't know why they can't hear the horn," he said to Carmen.

"What are we going to do?"

"I don't know. We're in a tough spot. Let me think."

His entire life, he had been the man who finds the solution to the thorniest problem, who figures out how to do something everyone else said wasn't possible. The idea of admitting defeat was foreign to him, but he didn't see any way of surviving outside the Chrysler, and they would not survive much longer inside. The interior temperature was rising. The house just in front of them and the trees and vegetation around them were burning furiously, and it wouldn't be long before the car caught fire. If he couldn't figure out what to do, he and his wife were going to burn with the Chrysler.

At that moment, a gust of wind swept through the lot, cleared out the smoke, and looking in the rearview mirror he saw the berm separating Dan's property from his neighbor's. Just over the berm was the northwest side of Dan's house, which meant the path along that side of the house to the backyard was about a forty-five-degree angle over his left shoulder, forty or fifty yards behind them. If they could reach that path, they could make it to the pool. The pool was full of water and set at a distance from the house. He recalled one large tree on the west side of the back-yard that he was sure was on fire. He calculated it was twenty-five yards from the point where they could enter the backyard to the edge of the pool. He scanned his memory for anything else that could block their path but he found nothing except fire and fear. Then he remembered there was a fence around the pool. It wasn't a huge obstacle, but he would need to figure out a way through it quickly. Armando turned to his wife. Determination had replaced fear. "I think there's only one thing we can do. We've got to go back to the pool."

He read Carmen's face and saw she was playing this out in her mind, mapping the route back for herself, though he knew she would let him lead the way.

"Okay. Good," she said.

He looked at her to gauge how well this plan was settling with her. He could see she was scared, but he could also see she was as determined as he was.

"Ready?" he asked.

"Yes," she said, looking down into her lap. She closed her eyes.

"Keep us safe, Father," he said.

"Please, Lord," she added.

"Hold your breath before we get out."

"Okay."

"*Vamonos.*"

Armando and Carmen looked into each other's eyes, inhaled deeply, swung the car doors open, and tried to run.

Carmen stumbled getting out, and nearly fell to the ground but caught herself by bracing her right hand against the trunk of the Chrysler. She quickly recoiled. Touching the metal of the car was like touching a pot pulled straight from the stove. The entire area around the car was burning. Her hair, face, and the skin on her arms started to burn.

When Armando opened his door, flames rushed to feed on the oxygen in the car's cabin, scorched the left side of his face and his body, and, though he wouldn't realize it until later, set his pajamas on fire. He saw at a glance that the car had gotten stuck in a flower bed. Infuriating. He should have been able to get the car out of a flower bed. But it was too late. He'd gotten stuck. Luis and Monica were gone. He and Carmen were on their own.

He ran to the back of the car and grabbed Carmen's hand, and together they ran through the neighbor's burning yard toward Dan's house. The smoke was thick. They could barely see each other through it, much less the ground or a path to Dan's backyard. Light from the flames only contributed to the confusion, and the roar of the fire combined with falling tree limbs and exploding structures nearly overwhelmed him. He wondered how Carmen was handling this. If she would be okay. As if reading his mind, she squeezed his hand, signaling she trusted him to guide her.

Neither of them could see through the smoke, but years of hunting had taught Armando how to track a target in any condition. He knew they were headed in the right direction, but he didn't know if they would get there in time. Carmen ran right next to him. He could smell her burning hair and flesh. They scrambled up a slight incline and reached the berm separating the two properties. Less than ten feet from the east side of Dan's property was a massive body of fire stretching to the north side of the house. Along the berm to their left, trees blazed. To their right, the berm was too high to cross, and beyond that was the valley. Somehow, they had come to the only passable point in the border between Dan's home and his neighbor. In minutes, the fire would hit Dan's house, and if he and Carmen weren't in the backyard, they'd be trapped. In a flash, he took in the miserable irony before them: what had been the most dangerous place in the world ten minutes ago was the only safe place left.

Together, they crossed the berm and onto the side yard on the southwest side of Dan's house. He gestured Carmen toward the pool in the far south corner of the lot. Already it looked like a substantial amount of water had been lost when the radiant heating system exploded. The system had housed much of the pool's water, and when the system blew, the water went with it. Enough water, in fact, that the pool looked less promising, but it was the only hope they had. He locked around at the amount of destruction wrought in just a handful of minutes since they had left. Armando was astonished to see everything surrounding the house was now burning, and he estimated they had less than a minute before Dan's house caught fire. If they didn't get in the pool now, they would die.

He raised his foot and kicked at the privacy fence bordering the pool. The gate, weakened from the heat, flew apart, splintering under the force of his kick. He noticed the fence breaking was barely audible over the wind and fire roaring around them. Whatever happened next, it was going to happen at the end of Crystal Court, on top of this hill.

He yelled to Carmen as they ran toward the pool. "When we jump in, stay underwater for as long as possible! Expose as little skin as you can! Don't let go of my hand!"

They jumped hand-in-hand into the deep end of the pool. The pain of the water hitting their charred skin was extreme. As they plunged beneath the surface, the water vibrated with the shock of a powerful explosion. The explosion was immediately followed by a ceiling of flame that ripped overhead. *That's got to be Dan's propane tank*, Armando thought. He and Carmen held their breath.

The harsh sting from the initial pain turned to a pulsing throb under the water. It didn't feel better, but it felt less life-threatening. He prayed the flames would subside before they had to come up for air.

Pain swallowed his left arm. Carmen clung to his right arm, struggling to keep her entire body underneath the water. Both rose to the surface just enough to pull black, smoke-filled air through their noses and mouths. The water was surprisingly cold.

*This pool was the only reason he and Carmen were still alive.* Some might call it luck that they had escaped their car and found their way back. Armando wouldn't, and Carmen certainly wouldn't. God had touched them. God had given him the idea to come to the pool, and it must also have been God who allowed him to find the one clear path back to Dan's house. How else to explain the smoke clearing at the exact moment he looked in the rearview mirror and at the only place in the berm he and Carmen could have gotten through? Had he taken a different route, they would have been surrounded by flames and perished. But that's not how it happened, because that's not where God led them. Maybe it was sheer luck they made it to the pool, but as Armando submerged himself, and the cold water enveloped his body, he knew God had played a role in getting them this far.

Armando raised his head slowly above the water. He and Carmen had not spoken since they jumped into the pool together. They had to survive the night, and he wanted her to conserve her energy. He assumed she was thinking about their children, their grandchildren, and Luis. He was sure she was praying the family had gotten down the mountain to safety, and that she would live to see them again.

Armando turned his attention back to the house he and his family had been sleeping in just fifteen minutes earlier. It was completely engulfed in flames. He looked to the west, across the valley, and saw the entire hillside was burning. The earth vibrated from a distant explosion; Armando turned his gaze to the east, and saw a massive fireball rise like a ghastly firework above a house still clinging to the hill. He wondered who lived there. None of the homes this high in the canyon had natural gas lines running to them. Each relied on a large propane tank, and as the fire advanced, he knew the tanks would explode, just as Dan's had, just as the one at the house across the hill had. He turned toward Carmen. She, too, was staring at the hillside. There was no way of knowing if anyone was going to be safe, including themselves.

It was about 12:45 a.m. The acrid smoke burned Armando's eyes and dried out his throat. He knew Carmen's lungs were already strained from the lack of oxygen. Surrounded by flames and with nowhere else to go, they worked out a routine to survive the night. He held her to him. Carmen rested her head on his shoulder, and together, they moved toward the deepest end of the pool, away from the flames destroying the house.

When they reached the end of the pool, he gripped the edge tightly with his charred left hand and supported his wife with his right.

"Dear God, bring us and our family safely through this," she prayed.

"Amen," he whispered.

Then he gave the signal, and they both went back under the water.

# Luis 1:OO a.m.

LUIS FELT SICK TO HIS STOMACH AS HE GOT OUT OF THE car. His eyes scoured the road, looking for the Chrysler. The relief of seeing Monica and Arielle drive through the wall of flames in the Audi was snuffed out completely when Armando and Carmen hadn't driven through behind them.

As he approached the Audi, he saw Monica was on her phone, and he knew she was trying to reach her mother. He could see by the look on her face she wasn't getting through. He knew his wife well enough to see the frustration on her face and fear in her body language. For some reason, Carmen wasn't answering her phone, and that could only mean something bad.

Monica opened the door and stepped out, reeling in a circle, shaking the phone in her hand like it was a weapon failing her when she needed it most. Everything around them was burning out of control, but Luis hardly noticed.

"Where are they? Her phone is just going to voicemail!" she shouted. Her face was wet with tears.

Luis shook his head; he didn't have the words he needed right now. "I don't know. They should have been right behind you. Did you see them?"

"No! When I turned, I thought he did, too. Driving down, I couldn't see anything behind me. The smoke was too thick. Where do you think they went?"

"I don't know, but I'm going to find out," he said.

"What are you going to do?"

"I'm gonna go back and find them."

"Oh my God," she said. "I wanna go. They're my parents."

"You can't," Luis said as gently and calmly as he could. "You just can't."

Monica groaned.

"I will go, and I will be back."

Luis knew this was not what Monica wanted, and he couldn't be sure leaving her to drive down alone was the right thing, but if he stood there any longer, he would feel complicit in the worst thing that could happen to her parents. With no good option and no way to not take action, the only thing left to do was get started.

"Take Arielle and wait for me at the bottom. Please. Go."

Monica threw her arms to the ground, spun herself around, and got back in the Audi, closing the door harder than necessary.

She put her palm to the side window and looked at him.

Luis brought both hands to his lips, clasped his hands together, and extended his arms toward her. He mouthed the word "Go."

Monica's shoulders sagged, and she stepped back out of the car and walked toward him.

He wrapped her in his arms.

"Promise me you'll be careful."

"I will. I promise you I will. Go," Luis said, knowing full well driving back up the road was going to be insanely dangerous. "If we get separated, find a way to get to Joel and Shannon's. I'll meet you there as soon as I can."

Joel and Shannon's house was the only safe place he could think of to send them. It made sense for her to go with Arielle, and he could see she understood. It was also plain to see that the idea of leaving him and her parents behind was agonizing.

"I can't leave them!" she cried.

"You have to! There's no other way!" He stood in the road facing her. He was not getting into the Explorer until Monica was in the Audi and driving Arielle down the road and off the mountain.

She didn't move.

"Monica, please!" He wrapped his arms around her again. "You have to go. You need to get Ari out of here. I need you to be safe. Please." He dreaded to think of Monica and Arielle navigating their way to Petaluma on their own through the fire, through street closures, chaos, and God knows what else. His worry was tempered by the small comfort of knowing they would be heading away from the danger, not back into it.

"I don't want to leave," Monica said, and her voice cracked.

Luis held her tightly. He didn't want to let go. The thought of her leaving and driving down this burning mountain on her own shattered him. "I need you to go," he said. "I can't go look for them until I know you're getting out of here."

He kissed her. He wondered if it would be the last time. Monica would tell him later she wondered the same thing. "I love you," he whispered.

"Come back to me. Promise me you'll come back," Monica said. Her body was shaking. Luis might have held her longer, but he was hyper-aware that everything around them was on fire, and they were losing time.

"I will, I promise. Now please get going. I'll see you at Joel and Shannon's."

Luis didn't want to let Monica go, but he did. He knew driving back up the mountain was suicide, but he couldn't abandon her parents up there. He watched as she got in the Audi and drove slowly down the road, then he turned back to the Explorer.

LUIS CRINGED AS HE APPROACHED EVERY BEND IN THE road, wondering what he'd find when he rounded it. He eased his foot slightly off the gas, knowing he might have to hit the brake suddenly. He was glad no one was following him; it made driving easier. He wondered where that fire truck was. His hands and arms ached from gripping the wheel so tightly, from the tension of being poised to avoid danger.

The one thing he had going for him as he made his way back up the hill was the wind was now at his back, and he didn't have embers flying into his windshield. Smoke still billowed around him, but it moved with him, not against him. Occasionally Luis would find a clear pocket he could follow for a few yards. Nothing about the drive was smooth. It was still a suicide mission, but he was relieved to find it easier than going down had been.

Something hit the roof of the car with a thump. Luis jumped and yanked his foot off the gas. A flaming branch, at least ten feet long, fell on the roof of the car, bounced onto the hood, then rolled off the driver's side. He pressed the gas, praying the branch wouldn't cause a problem on the way back down.

*If there is a way back down.*

He passed what had been the burning pickup, now just a char-coal husk, its mangled metal barely recognizable. He inhaled sharply, knowing the wall of fire they'd driven through was just ahead of him.

*It's my fault they're up here. I have to find them. I can't go back to Monica without her parents.*

He was sick with fear and worry. It had been his friend's house, and his suggestion to stay there. He knew the odds were strong that Monica's parents were already dead. He knew the rational thing would be to turn back, but guilt pushed him forward.

He felt the bump-bump-bump of the Explorer's tires hitting the raised dots of the centerline. He was losing the middle of the road. Visibility had dropped. Slowly, carefully, he corrected course. Sweat dripped off him. It stung his eyes and drenched his clothes. He was back in the thick of the fire.

*I can't leave them to die up here.*

*I can't leave them to die up here.*

Suddenly, a groaning sounced from the left side of the road, and the earth shuddered beneath him. Luis swerved to the right to avoid a huge tree as it fell into the street and over the left lane. Once he'd passed it, he returned to the centerline.

*God, help me make it back to Monica*, he prayed as branches from neighboring trees began to fall. Sparks flew everywhere, showering the Explorer's hood. He just hoped none made their way inside the engine block.

Just ahead of him, he saw two uprooted trees on either side of the road. Their uppermost branches intertwined, forming an arch large enough for even the Explorer to drive through comfortably. To Luis, the trees called to mind two lovers straining to embrace one another over a great distance. Flames danced along the bark, creating a ring that had likely been the twenty-foot-tall wall of flames they'd driven through earlier.

He gunned the engine and sped through the opening then slowed quickly before turning into the next curve. The heat in the car had increased substantially, and he felt himself getting woozy.

*Keep it together. Just a little bit longer. Do it for Monica. Get through this alive.*

# Monica 1:00 a.m.

I watched Luis get into the car, then waited for a moment before I ran back to the Audi through the roar and the heat of the world burning around us and got in. Arielle was on her phone, sobbing. I knew she was talking to Dennis. I shut the door, but it didn't deaden the noise. The noise was in my ears. I looked out the windshield. Ash and embers covered the hood and windshield. I'd seen trees falling around me, and now it was as if a tree had fallen across my chest. Luis was going to die, trying to rescue my parents. What have I done? Oh my God, what have I just done? My body started to shake. I couldn't stop it. My husband was going to die, and I couldn't stop it.

"Hold on," Arielle said into the phone. "What's happening? Where are Abu and Abi? Where is Luis going?"

I took a deep breath, put the car in drive, and tried to sound calm.

"He's going back to look for them. They didn't follow us down."

"WHAT?"

"Is that Dennis on the phone?"

"Yes! Where are we going?"

I took my foot off the brake. The car moved forward. I passed Luis in the Explorer and looked into his face. He was beautiful. He smiled at me, pointed down the road, and mouthed the words, "I love you."

The Audi inched past him. I watched in the rearview mirror as he swung the Explorer in the other direction. Its taillights disappeared into the smoke.

"We're driving to Joel and Shannon's. Luis will find Mamá and Papá and bring them there to join us."

"Oh, my God."

"Ari, I need you to stay calm. We still have to get down from here. Please be calm, baby."

She relayed this latest news to Dennis.

I dialed my brother's cell. I needed to hear his voice and let him know what was happening. He didn't pick up. I dialed his landline and let it ring. When he answered, he sounded groggy. I told him where we were and what was happening. I couldn't tell him everything without losing it, but I had to tell him about our parents. He needed to know they were lost. Between gasping for air to keep from bawling into the phone, I told him Luis was going back to look for them. I tried to keep it together, to not completely freak my little brother out, but I was probably barely coherent. Then I saw a fire truck, told my brother I needed to go, and hung up.

I pulled over and jumped out of the car. "Help me!" I shouted, pointing up the hill.

A firefighter approached. "Ma'am, I need you to evacuate this area."

"My mom and dad . . ." That was all I could get out.

He looked at me with concern.

"My mom and dad . . ."

"Where are they?"

I noticed the name on his coat: Jason Novak. "At the end of Crystal Court—the last house. We left, but we lost them. I don't know where they are."

Novak said, "I'll go up there and take a look."

"No! You don't understand! My parents are trapped up there!" I pointed up the road. My hand was shaking, almost uncontrollably. "They were driving behind us, but they didn't make it down the hill. My husband, his name is Luis, just went back up to try and find them." When I mentioned Luis's name, I began crying.

"We're heading up that way, and we will do our best to find them," Novak said, "but you need to get clear of this area. The wind keeps shifting, and the fire is headed back this way. Give me your name and phone number, and I will call you when I find them."

He handed me a notepad. I wrote down my name, Luis's name, my parents' names, and my phone number on it. "Thank you," I said, handing his notepad back to him. It seemed so futile.

"No problem, just get in the car and head to safety."

I nodded and ran back to the car. I took one more look up the road, asked God to watch over my family, and got back in the driver's seat.

I looked back at Arielle. "Ari? You okay?"

"I don't know. Yes," she said.

I wasn't convinced, but there was nothing to do or say at this point. We had to keep moving.

I started the car and headed down slowly. The road began to level out as we approached the valley floor. It looked like everything below us was also on fire, but seeing the fire truck had given me a sense that I'd passed through the worst of it. Smoke still made seeing the road difficult and frequently impossible, flaming branches still dropped onto the car from burning trees lining the street, and I drove through shower after shower of embers. Still, I was no longer afraid Arielle and I would become trapped and burn to death on this road.

In minutes, we reached Riebli Road. Riebli runs east-west and is the main access route for all the smaller roads which snake through the surrounding hills. It's also the primary artery leading to larger southbound roads into the city of Santa Rosa and, ultimately, Highway 101.

It was bedlam: a smoke-filled, teeming mass of vehicles, jammed bumper-to-bumper, trying to flee the blaze. I turned the wheel to the right and inched my way into the stream of westbound cars and trucks. We were on flat ground but moving slower than when I'd been driving blindly downhill through the smoke. I screamed in frustration. My hands clenched and unclenched the steering wheel, seeking some kind of release from the frustration and bewilderment. That's when I noticed I wasn't wearing my wedding ring.

I must have left it in the bathroom at the house. I had to bite down on my lip to keep from crying because I knew if I started crying, I would lose it. Staring at my bare finger, I thought, *What if Luis doesn't make it? Is this an omen? It's not an omen. That's stupid.* My head did this dance for a couple of minutes before the dance moved into the pit of my stomach, which began to curdle.

I wasn't done being a wife. I couldn't be a widow. A car surged forward in front of me, cutting off two other cars in the process. Horns blared as they swerved to avoid it.

We'd made it through the fire, and now we were going to die at the intersection of Wilshire and Riebli because some idiot broadsides us.

I tried to breathe deeply to calm myself, but I just choked on the smoke that still filled the car. By now, the scent was burned into the upholstery, and it was never going to come out. I glanced in the rearview mirror, half-expecting to see the fire sweeping up behind us, reaching out for us with its deadly tendrils. We escaped it once, and it was unlikely to let us go a second time.

*What about Luis?* I thought, feeling my anxiety ratchet up even tighter. *What if it catches him and doesn't let him go this time? What about my mom? My dad? What happened to them? How could they have made it if they weren't behind us? What do I do if they—STOP! STOP! STOP!*

Suddenly I felt as if I were going to faint. My breathing became shallow. I was taking quick, gasping breaths. I was about to have a panic attack.

Then I heard Arielle sobbing in the backseat. I forced myself to be strong for my daughter. I leaned back in the seat, breathed in slowly, fought the cough, and started to bring myself back from the ledge.

I took another deep breath and let it ease out of me.

"You okay, baby?"

Arielle sniffled but didn't answer.

*Of course, she isn't okay. I'm not okay. But we will be. No matter what happens, we will be. No, I don't know if I'll ever be okay again. I just don't know.*

One thing at a time. That was all I could focus on. If I had to focus on more than one, I'd go crazy. Another guy tired of waiting zoomed through the intersection, narrowly missing another car.

*Just get through this intersection. We'll figure out the next step after that. The important thing is to get through this, and then we'll tackle the next step.*

Finally, we cleared the intersection. I drove another block and then pulled into the parking lot of a gas station. I wanted to call Luis. I wanted to hear some kind of assurance we were going to be okay. I had my phone in my hand and was about to call him when I realized the stupidity and selfishness of what I was about to do. *He doesn't need a phone call to distract him. He needs me to be safe.*

I put the phone down, put the Audi into drive and headed back out into the smoke-filled darkness, praying I would soon see Luis and my parents.


AT LAST, AFTER DRIVING EVERY TINY BACKROAD, LOOKING for a way to a freeway that wasn't blocked, screaming at the GPS on my phone, which kept sending us into the fire, I managed to squeeze my way onto the 101 Interstate. Finally, I was headed for Joel and Shannon's house in Petaluma. I recognized I should feel grateful to be alive and to have my daughter with me in the car headed to safety. Instead, all I thought about was what a horrible wife and daughter I was, leaving my husband to find my parents we had left stranded on a burning mountainside. The fire was consuming Sonoma. Guilt consumed me.

I needed Luis here.

I prayed he would find them alive and safe, and be able to bring them safely down. If he didn't . . . or couldn't . . . . Well, I didn't want to even think about that, but if the worst had already happened, I hoped he got himself out and came to me as fast as possible. The uncertainty of not knowing where anyone was or what they were facing was like someone stomping on my ribcage. It hurt to breathe, to think. I could actually feel pain knifing through my chest around my heart.

Arielle was still gently crying in the backseat. I needed to offer her comfort, despite my fears, despite my doubts. "Everything's going to be okay, baby. We're all going to be okay."

# Armando y Carmen 1:00 a.m.

*Wildlife biologist and falconer Monte Kirven, age 81, dies in his home on Linda Lane off Mark West Springs Road.*

ARMANDO COULD BARELY FEEL HIS FINGERS AS THEY gripped the edge of the concrete. From the southwest corner of the pool, he and Carmen watched the house rapidly disintegrate in flames. It had been a magnificent house, and he would not have believed something so well-built could burn so fast, but he watched how the fire moved and realized the open floor plan helped the fire spread more quickly than it would have in a more traditional home. The heat and smoke produced by the fire were enough to make breathing a sheer act of will. He could see his wife was having a harder time of it than he was. They had been keeping as much of their heads underwater as possible, letting only their lips and noses break the surface to get oxygen as needed. Still, the sensation of being underwater while breathing had been disorienting, and they'd had to peek their heads out repeatedly to reorient themselves and see what was happening around them.

Once they'd plunged into the water, they physically let go of one another only for the briefest moments. Every body part except their mouths and noses might be submerged, and their eyes closed to protect them from embers, but he knew where Carmen was at all times, and she knew where he was. They'd come too far, been together too long to let go of each other now. Together they were strong. They had always been strong together. As the world burned, Armando remembered this, and it gave him the courage to not surrender.

There was a sudden roar as a support beam crashed to the ground, causing flames to shoot out from the house toward the pool with the force of a blowtorch. They pulled their heads back underwater. Carmen gripped his arms tightly. The brightness of the flames passing overhead was nearly blinding.

The only way out of this was to stay put and wait it out. Eventually, the fire would burn everything on the property to ashes, the swimming pool would remain largely intact, and if they could wait it out, safely, they might be able to walk out of there. Armando was also aware there were many things that could kill them even here in the pool. He made a checklist of potentially lethal dangers: tank explosions, fire, projectiles, asphyxiation, hypothermia, heart attacks, landslides, and even animals. Black bears and mountain lions were not uncommon in the Sonoma hills.

By nature and training, he was used to looking at situations from every angle, identifying alternative ways to achieve the desired outcome and the potential obstacles to achieving success. This ability had served him well in business. Now he found himself identifying every possible way he and his wife could die. He stopped himself from focusing on these negative thoughts and concentrated on the immediate, painfully simple solution: stay in the pool, avoid all dangers, maintain physical strength, and wait.

He had no idea how long that could take, or even what time it was, but he knew daylight was still many hours away.

When his concentration faltered, he prayed.

When he needed to think of something positive, he went back to his youth with Carmen, remembering how they met on the phone, what she was like the first day he knocked on her door, and how mature and poised she seemed compared to other girls her age. He thought about how she made him laugh, and that led him down a path of trying to recall the funniest things she had done and said during their decades together. He recalled her best jokes, who was present when she told them, and the sound of their laughter. Carmen was a good storyteller; her timing and delivery were always spot on. Her mother had told him how Carmen would go to the Monserrate to eavesdrop on the people in the lobby or the bar. The Monserrate attracted a wide array of characters, many of them connected to mobsters, ubiquitous in certain parts of Havana, and Carmen would listen to their stories, which were often outrageous tales of double-dealing, infidelity, and the settling of scores. She could tell, just by how these men spoke (and it was always men), that many of their stories were well-embellished if not outright lies, but she loved eavesdropping on them. For her, it was like listening in on forbidden gossip, and those hours sitting just out of view but listening attentively taught her how to spin a yarn herself and how to spot a fake one. Both skills had played a part in her later successes in her professional career.

Armando realized early on that Carmen had an innate ability to absorb an incredible amount of detail, and she put it to use in myriad ways that continued to surprise him throughout their life together. She remembered names and birthdays and favorite colors. She could recall entire meals in restaurants they ate in decades before, including the server. She knew exactly how long it had been since she last spoke to someone and everything they discussed. She absorbed every nuance of a face, and once she knew it, she could read a person's mood in a flash. And Carmen put this skill to use for the people who mattered to her. She used it to enrich their lives and to let them know how much they meant to her.

In Cuba, the older men, the wiser ones at least, would counsel the younger ones to find a woman who made them a better man. Armando knew Carmen Caldentey made him a better man. He had always been proud to be beside her. He'd been proud to introduce her to new friends and associates as his wife. She was the inspiration and motivation for every success he achieved during their life together. She gave his life purpose and direction. God had brought them together all those years ago specifically to have this life they had lived together.

Now they were facing the most immediate danger they'd ever experienced in more than fifty years of marriage. They were trapped in the middle of a wildfire with no way out, and at the center of their predicament was a test of their faith.

He would do everything he could to keep both of them alive.

Armando thought of his parents and wondered what would have happened to them in similar circumstances. He was sure it would have quickly devolved into each assigning blame to the other.

His lungs were aching, burning with the need for oxygen, and he knew his wife's must be, too. He raised his lips slightly above the waterline and began to gasp and cough. Beside him, Carmen did the same. Even though they were standing in cold water, the heat from the fire heated the air around them to an unbearable degree. Furnace-hot winds, gusting at sixty miles an hour, blasted their skin. The flames, like tentacles of a beast, reached out to devour everything within their grasp. They generated their own wind, like small tornados, and Armando gasped in surprise as one of the heavy deck chairs was lifted in the wind and flung over the pool and into the canyon. Another chair followed the first and barely missed hitting them. "We have to stay under as much as we can," he said, his voice raspy.

"I know," Carmen whispered, drawing as deep a breath as she could.

They ducked beneath the water moments before the rest of the furniture went flying overhead. For a moment, Armando was sure some of it would land on top of them, and he struggled to pull them along the edge, further out of danger. Miraculously, none of the furniture hit the pool but sailed over the edge of the backyard and into the canyon below.

When they came up again for air, he could see his wife's face was strained, and she looked afraid. "Just hold on to me," he whispered.

The weight of Carmen's hands on his arms was familiar, comforting. There was a tension in them, though, that he had not felt in a long time, and for some reason, this reminded him of the first dance they'd shared. Armando closed his eyes.

He was thirteen, and he was nervous in a way he didn't know people could be nervous. Everything in him knew he belonged to her, and he prayed she felt the same. Her hands were soft yet strong. It would be a few years before she would qualify for the Olympic volleyball team, but she was already a capable athlete. He put his arm around her waist and danced as close to her as he dared. He leaned forward slightly, and she did as well. His heart stammered as she pressed her cheek softly to his. He wanted to hold on to that moment forever. On the dance floor, the song ended, but in his heart, it never did.

# Luis 1:20 a.m.

Luis was in trouble. The fires were still raging heavily, and they grew in violence and intensity as he drove up the road. He was certain Armando and Carmen were already gone, but he had to know for sure. As long as there was even the tiniest chance they were still alive, he had to do everything he could to find them and bring them to safety.

The night and the smoke and the fire made the road an apocalyptic landscape. He had no idea how far he'd driven or if he was anywhere near the top of the hill. He was completely disoriented, and the only thing keeping him from driving off the side was seeing the yellow stripe from time to time and feeling the braille of the elevated bumps under his tires when he strayed off it. He would turn the wheel, putting all of his trust in a sixth sense that seemed to govern the relationship between his hands and the steering wheel. He came to a part of the road he didn't recognize and was startled when the wheels suddenly drove over bumps. The curve was shallower than he had anticipated. He corrected to get the car back on track. Luis thought he had somehow made a wrong turn into someone's driveway before he realized he was on the last stretch of road before it leveled out at the top of the hill. Directly to his left were trees and brush, fuel for the fire. Two hundred feet ahead was the narrow fork leading up to Dan's house, or what would be left of it.

Luis inched slowly forward. He was almost there.

He hadn't gone more than a few feet when the smoke parted, and he could see the road. He yelped and slammed the brakes. A downed tree lay across the road. It burned furiously. Flames snapped at the air around it. He leaned forward in the Explorer's driver's seat for a moment, staring ahead, then screamed in frustration. Less than a few hundred feet away, just on the other side of that burning tree, was the spot where he had last seen Monica's parents. He strained to see through the smoke and the flame for any sign of the Chrysler, but he could see nothing past the burning tree.

His eyes teared against the smoke in the cab and the sweat from his face. He rapidly blinked, trying to clear them, then wiped his face with his shirt. Finally, he could see a little better. What he saw confirmed his worst fears.

There was no way forward.

All around the car, bits of fiery debris and ash rained down. Flaming branches dropped on either side, effectively narrowing the road to a strip of asphalt not much wider than the Explorer. He looked in the rearview. Flames had closed in behind the Explorer.

There was no room to turn around in.

He thought *I'm going to die up here, too.*

Luis sat in the car for a moment, letting the truth of his current circumstances sink in. There was too much fire and debris on the road to turn around. *I'm up here, they're up here, and the three of us are up here, and that's it.*

He didn't want to die, but he knew he had trapped himself. Heat from the flames radiated through the windows making the air inside the Explorer frighteningly difficult to breathe. He figured he had less than a minute before the fire surrounding him took hold of the Explorer, and it would be all over. He would have to find a way out immediately, but he barely had the strength to grip the wheel.

He thought of Monica, of their life together, and how their marriage had brought him such joy. They hadn't had nearly enough time together. He thought of all they planned to do in the future.

*She's waiting for me at Joel and Shannon's. I promised her I would come back.*

He was going to find a way to get down the hill even if he had to make a twenty-seven-point turn to do it. He shifted into reverse. He inched back and then forward, shifting and then nudging the car as fast as he could. He backed into a pile of flaming branches and his breath caught, waiting just a second to see if they would set the car on fire.

They didn't, and he quickly inched forward again, then back. The smoke and the constant tearing up of his eyes made it nearly impossible to keep track of where he was. He started coughing uncontrollably. He saw a downed tree directly in front of him, and for a terrible second, he thought he had overturned and done a complete circle. Then relief swept through him. It was a different tree, one along the side of the road. He was halfway through where he needed to be to point the nose of the car down the hill. An explosion shook the ground, and more flaming branches fell around him. Luis imagined the fire was a monster he was fighting against for his life, and that gave him the energy to push forward and win. He wouldn't let it kill him, as it had killed Monica's parents.

He would beat the monster and drive back to Monica. Luis shifted back and forth in a seemingly endless loop of drive, reverse, drive, reverse, drive, reverse. Each time he cranked the wheel as hard as he could to get the most out of each turn. He began to wonder how much longer the Explorer would hold up. When would the tires give out to the heat? How long before fire crept under the hood and the motor blew? He made another shift backward and pulled the gear shift back into drive. He had a path. It was narrow, and flaming debris was falling all around him, but he had a chance. He let out a gasp of relief, tapped the gas, and started down the mountain.

Luis drove as fast as he could without risking driving off the road. He was terrified he wouldn't make it down alive, but it had nothing to do with the homes or trees burning down around him. He was beginning to hallucinate. Where there had been flaming trees, there were monsters with flaming eyes and jaws ready to chase him down and swallow him whole. They wanted to kill him, but he wouldn't let them. Sometimes they looked like trees, and he would see one move like it was about to fall, and he'd swerve, but a second later, he'd realize it was the monsters trying to trick him into driving his car into a burning house or down the side of the hill.

He would beat this thing. He kept driving, swerving every few feet, but quickly returning to the center of the road, hugging it. Explosions from combusting propane tanks and homes shook the ground as he drove. A flaming branch dropped in front of him. He swerved, barely missing it, running over more debris in the process. The car jolted hard. *Keep going*, he coaxed, *don't die on me here.*

Finally, he made it to the place where he and Monica had stopped. Ahead of him, the wall of fire still blocked the road like hell's theater curtain.

Luis gently put the Explorer into park. Every option he had was a bad one. He stepped out of the car and stood on the road, letting the embers rain down on him. He had no idea what to do next.

Find his way down the hill, leaving the fate of Carmen and Armando a question mark that would haunt him forever?

Turn around and get them, even if it meant risking his life? But could he live with himself if he didn't try?

Both scenarios promised grief for Monica. Whichever one he chose, someone would die, and it would be his fault. He paced circles of frustration and despair on the smoke-filled road. Embers on the asphalt crunched beneath his feet. He tried to calm himself by taking a deep breath and choked on the smoke. For a moment, he thought he might collapse, but then a new sound split the air, and he turned around to see a fire engine coming up the road toward him, honking its horn.

The fire engine's arrival gave Luis a needed shot of optimism. Help was here.

Luis climbed back into the Explorer and pulled it out of the way, lining it up as far as he could along the side of the road. He was relieved to see help arrive, and for the first time that night, he had hope. *These guys will find them. It will be okay.*

Instead, the fire engine pulled past him and then stopped. Its motor kept running, creating a low rumble underneath the sound of the wind and the constant popping and groaning of the homes and trees burning around them.

A firefighter jumped down from the truck.

"You need to get out of here right now! It's not safe."

Luis stepped forward. 'Please, my wife's parents are up there. They were driving behind us, and we lost them. I just tried getting back up there to look for them, but there's a tree down across the road."

The firefighter strode forward. The name on his coat read Novak. "Are you Luis?"

"Yes," he said, surprised at the question.

"I met your wife, and she told me what was going on. Don't worry. I'll go up there, but you have to get out of here."

Luis nodded, blinking back tears. The fire engine lumbered slowly past him and began ascending the hill. He watched it go, impressed that its lights were still visible even through the smoke. He knew he should leave, but he watched as it lumbered further up the road. *The firefighters will find Armando and Carmen,* he thought. *They have to.*

The lights grew dimmer as the truck advanced up the mountain, but when he expected them to disappear, they didn't, and something inside Luis twitched painfully. It looked as if the truck had stopped. He squinted, trying to see what was going on, but he could only barely see the lights through the smoke, nothing else.

For a moment, nothing happened. Then, through the smoke, Luis saw the lights begin to move again, but instead of growing dimmer as the truck drove away, they grew brighter as the truck rolled back down the mountain.

Luis stood in the road and watched numbly as the truck slowly backed toward him and stopped at the spot it left just a minute before. The same firefighter, Novak, jumped down from the truck and walked up to him. His face was grim.

"We could only make it about a hundred and fifty yards. It's too intense. It's too heavy for me to take my guys in. We couldn't pass beyond it. I'm sorry. I'll try again, but we can't get up there right now."

Luis stared at Novak, horror and desperation churning in his gut. If a fire engine couldn't make it up the hill, what chance did Monica's parents have of making it down?

"Your wife told me she was heading to a friend's house in Petaluma. You should join her," Novak said.

"I can't. I can't show up there without them."

Novak insisted. "You need to get to safety and be with your wife."

"You don't understand. How am I supposed to go there and look her in the eyes and tell her I couldn't find them? That I have no idea where they are?"

Novak put a hand on Luis's shoulder and looked him in the eye. "I promise you, I will make sure I get up there, but you need to leave."

Luis nodded. Novak had an air of strength and confidence that was reassuring, Luis believed him.

"My name is Jason. Give me your cell number, and I'll call you the moment I know anything about them."

Luis did, grateful there was someone who might be able to help them.

"You've done all you can here. It's time to go," Novak said.

"Thank you," Luis said. He walked back to the Explorer and climbed into the cab. He wiped his eyes. It was over. He looked back at Novak and his crew parked just a few yards behind him. He hoped they were as capable as they appeared. He turned the key, shifted into drive, and drove slowly away.

# Monica 1:20 a.m.

I HAD TRIED CALLING MY MOTHER A DOZEN TIMES SINCE I left Luis, and every time it just rang and rang before going to voicemail. Every time I heard her voice, my heart leaped in a flash of hope, then fell. It was her outgoing greeting. Driving south-bound toward Petaluma on the 101 Interstate, I tried calling again. This time it didn't ring but went straight to voicemail. I felt like I was going to be sick. I called right back, just in case someone else was calling her at the same moment, perhaps my brother. Again, it went straight to voicemail. My mom was meticulous about keeping her phone charged, and this had only one explanation. The phone had been destroyed.

"No," I whispered.

My mind filled with horrific possibilities, but I kept telling myself it only meant Dan's house was gone; it didn't mean my parents were. I reminded myself that I'd looked when she came out of the house, and I hadn't seen her phone in her hand. She'd had nothing in her hands. She'd left it at Dan's, and it was gone. That's all.

Still, this new development laid bare the terrible fear I'd been trying to shut down ever since I looked back through the flames and realized my parents weren't behind me. Now it crawled along the edges of my mind, like a sickening spider, poisoning my thoughts. *What if I'd lost them? What was going to happen to Luis? What if I'd lost all three of them?*

The thought of losing Luis awoke a suffocating horror I wasn't equipped to contemplate. I fought it. I choked it down. Luis was level-headed and courageous. He had gotten Arielle and me safely down the hill, and he'd make it down again, this time with my parents. My father was a tower of strength, physically and mentally. My mom wasn't just competitive; she was a fighter. They'd do everything they could to survive. They wouldn't give up, and I couldn't give up on them.

Smoke billowed over the freeway, and ahead of me, orange lights flared in the darkness and grew brighter as I drove. There was a genuine possibility we were heading into another fire. What if there was nowhere to go? I'd put the fire behind us half an hour ago, and here it was again, looming in front of us. And this time, it was just the two of us.

Instead of worrying about Luis and my parents, I needed to start thinking about Arielle and how to keep us safe. But I felt lost. Literally. I was completely turned around and sure I was heading in the wrong direction. Somewhere in the smoke or in the chaos of trying to get on the freeway, I'd made a wrong turn. I glanced at the GPS on my phone. We were heading south, toward Petaluma.

And into another fire.

"Is that more fire?" Arielle gasped. She sounded terrified. "Yes," I said.

What I wanted to say was *No, Arielle. I'm sure they would have shut down the freeway if there was any danger*, but I wasn't sure of anything anymore.

Arielle and I watched in horror as fast-moving flames burned across the dry grass lining the opposite side of the highway, speeding toward the cars trying to escape the area. It was like watching a living, breathing dragon race across the ground and leap into the sky. It uprooted trees and tossed their flaming limbs aside as it advanced. I could feel the temperature of the air outside the car rise as it approached.

I wanted to run screaming from this, but all I could do was edge forward in the car, wishing the people in front of us would speed up or get out of my way, preferably both.

Firefighters converged onto the freeway, scrambling to slow the conflagration's increasing progress toward the road with great jets and plumes of water that disappeared inside the dragon's flaming maw. Perhaps my perception was born of fear, but the fire seemed to approach the firefighters with increasing speed as if rushing to meet its foes in battle.

I inhaled sharply and pressed on the gas, hoping the cars in front of me would do the same. They seemed oblivious to the approaching destruction. Some of the drivers appeared more curious than scared, fascinated by the scope and intensity of the scene erupting around them. I wanted to scream, but I didn't want to frighten Arielle any more than she already was. "Move, move, move," I whispered under my breath, wishing I could toss aside the cars ahead of us. "You don't know. You don't want to know. Just drive!"

I knew, and I didn't want to die because people's morbid fascination with destruction kept them from getting their feet off their brakes when they should be flooring the gas pedal.

Suddenly, finally, there was movement. A group of cars surged forward. I went with them, gasping as the heat of the fire grew. I didn't know how Luis and my parents were going to make it to Petaluma through a freeway sure to be burned down or closed down at any moment. They'd be forced to find another way out through the chaos of angry, snarled bottlenecks on any remaining routes, while everything around them burned. I wasn't even sure if we were going to make it through to Joel and Shannon's house. With each passing second, it was increasingly probable the fire would trap us all on the freeway. Everyone would have to abandon their cars and flee on foot. I wondered how many, like Arielle, weren't even wearing shoes. Most of us would probably die before making our way to safety.

I tried to calm myself with deep, steady breaths, but I couldn't keep my attention on breathing and still navigate through the cars around us. Nearly everyone was blaring their horns and driving aggressively into any open spot, trying to move forward. Everyone seemed scared. Violence felt imminent.

We went a hundred yards, two hundred. Three. Heat radiated into the car. I heard a roaring behind me and looked in the rearview mirror just in time to see the flaming dragon leap into the sky, soar over the top of the freeway, and crash to the ground on our side of the road. Now the fire blazed on both sides of the freeway, spewing flames onto cars and their hapless occupants.

Cars on every side of us slowed. I looked around and was horrified to realize the slow-down was caused by people easing off the gas to watch the world burn. They were actually mesmerized by the fire raging around them. A drive-thru inferno.

"Move!" I screamed. Not that they could hear me. I could barely hear myself over the growing din of sirens, honking horns, wind, and the churning flames. Smoke billowed over my head. I saw an opening in the middle lane and rocketed toward it. I didn't come this far to be trapped and killed.

But the flames kept pace with us, racing southbound on both sides of the freeway just behind us. Once again, the dragon mocked me, taunted me, dared me to try and escape it. No matter what I did or where I went, it would find me, and it would destroy my family and me.

# Armando y Carmen 1:30 a.m.

*Larry Broderick, age 51, is awakened by a neighbor at 1:30. His wife and three boys evacuate while he stays behind trying to save their Flintwood Drive home. He is unsuccessful and perishes in the neighborhood where he had lived since the age of five.*

ARMANDO COULD TELL HIS WIFE'S ARMS WERE ACHING BY how tightly she held on to him. Periodically, one or more of her fingers would become numb, and she would flex them to get the blood circulating again without taking her hand from him. It was hard for her to do, and he knew it hurt. She said numerous times, "I'm sorry I'm squeezing. I don't mean to," and she would loosen her grip on him slightly. Carmen had strong hands and arms.

"It doesn't hurt," Armando said softly.

She looked into his face and smiled. "Nothing hurts you, Mandi."

"One thing did."

"I remember," she said. There in the pool, with the fire still raging around them, Carmen closed her eyes and put her forehead on Armando's shoulder. "I remember all of it. But we've been so fortunate, Mandi."

"Yes. We have," he said.

Just then, the wind kicked up again in a ferocious blast, and Carmen lifted her head from Armando's shoulder. She knew what came next.

"Ready?" Armando asked.

Carmen nodded, and together they plunged under the water, leaving just their noses and mouths above. They'd stopped trying to hold their breath underwater; it had become too difficult, and they needed to conserve their strength. Instead, they exposed as little of themselves to the fire sweeping over their heads. The smoke and the heat ravaged their throats, their nasal passages, and their lungs, and he began to wonder how long they could last, or if help would arrive in time.

They surfaced again but had to go right back under as the wind gathered force once again. Over and over. The fire had reached a new level of intensity, whipped into a fury by eighty mile an hour winds. Dan's house was completely gone, but all around them, other houses and trees were burning, combusting, and smoke kept rising from the valley floor and hillside beneath them.

Eventually, the fire subsided enough that they thought they could keep their heads above the water again, and they clung together in the corner of the pool.

"*¡Pase, set, remate!*" Armando said.

"*Siempre,*" Carmen said.

The skin of Armando's face felt tight and raw. He knew it must be badly burned, but one thing had hurt him worse than this. He remembered how just months into their married life, Carmen suffered a miscarriage during her first pregnancy. She had tried to explain to him this often happened to new brides in Cuba, but he had never seen this happen to anyone in his family, and he didn't know that it happened in other families. She had responded by taking it in stride and moving forward. He had responded with grief he didn't know how to deal with, so he hadn't. Carmen would occasionally bring up the child in her prayers or wonder aloud about who or what their child might have become, especially as Carmen Teresa, Monica, and Armando Jr. grew. Armando, for his part, refused to think of it for decades. There weren't many problems in his life he had not solved for himself. Before he was ten years old, he had found freedom from his unhappy parents in the outdoors. As teenagers, he and Carmen had withstood years of opposition from people determined to keep them apart. Her miscarriage had been the biggest trial of their marriage. It was the first problem he had faced, which they could neither understand nor solve. It had been a crushing experience for him, but he had learned that a more positive, life-affirming response to such problems is to accept them as unfinished business and move forward.

The wind changed direction. It blew from the southeast and carried with it more smoke and the sound of explosions. Automobiles, transformers, propane tanks. Carmen, on his left, struggled to breathe. They needed to move to another part of the pool where the air was better.

Armando turned and looked at his wife.

Carmen looked back at him and relaxed her grip. "Does it hurt?" she asked.

"Not anymore."

Armando shook his head and gestured toward an area a few feet closer to where Dan's house had stood.

Carmen knew the signal. She nodded, and her grip on his arm tightened.

Armando pushed off, and slowly, gently, he moved them to their next spot. He knew if they survived, it would be because of Carmen's strength and God's mercy, and he trusted in both completely.

# Luis 1:30 a.m.

BY THE TIME LUIS MADE IT TO THE BOTTOM OF THE HILL, where Wilshire met Riebli Road, he could see the fire wasn't just behind him; it was burning in every direction. The most direct route to the 101 Interstate was to the right, but that way had been blocked off. He turned left, heading away from the route he knew, driving down Riebli in a direction he'd never gone before. An explosion in the distance caused him to jerk the wheel, nearly crashing the car into a pole. A fireball erupted in the sky as a building in the distance went up. It rattled him, and for a moment he lost his bearings. He looked up at the street signs as he approached an intersection and remembered where he was: on Riebli, heading east. The freeway was to the southwest. If he made a right turn, he would either find it eventually or drive in concentric circles until he hit a dead end. He remembered there was a parkway skirting the eastern side of a golf course south of Dan's. He drove further down Riebli, trying to figure out how to access it. If he could find the parkway, it would lead him to the freeway, and maybe there would be less traffic on it. Along the way, he saw and heard one explosion after another, as propane tanks throughout the valley exploded under the fire's relentless march. Each one assaulted his ears and vibrated destruction in his bones.

Luis replayed over and over what he would say to Monica when he showed up without her parents, even though he knew words could not possibly make things all right. The longer he drove without finding his way to the freeway, the more convinced he was that he should just go back to the firemen and try to help with the search. At least he would be doing something.

Fire raced down the street to Luis's right, and he sped forward, trying to stay ahead of it. He made a quick turn only to see a wall of flames spring up in front of the car. He turned again, driving as fast as he could on increasingly dark and narrow roads. There were no streetlights, which made him nervous. He was heading east into a less developed part of the county. He took a couple of more turns, trying to angle back west, in the direction of the freeway.

He passed a car that had been driven into a ditch and abandoned. A few hundred feet later, he drove past two more. The empty road stretched before him was littered with cars in the ditches that lined the street. *Where are the people who were driving them?* he wondered. The sky was bright orange and red from the fires that raged across the valley, and far above was the black night, obscured in smoke. Luis was no longer sure if he was driving away from the fire or right into it. His hands began to hurt from clutching the steering wheel.

He came to an intersection, looked to the left, and could see signs of civilization. He turned, heading south, grateful to be off the country road. He heard another explosion and tightened his grip on the steering wheel. *I should find a way back. I need to go back up the hill. Maybe the fire has died down enough that I can help find them.*

Novak had told him to go. He had also promised he would make it to the top of the hill and that he'd call the second he knew anything. The best thing Luis could do was trust Novak and do what he said. Luis knew all this on a rational level, but it didn't change the helplessness and shame that tormented him the further he drove from the mountain. He didn't want to go back without Monica's parents. He was also sure they were no longer alive. He knew Monica would be frantic until she heard from him. But if he called, he had nothing to tell her. He saw the 101 Interstate ahead. He should enter the southbound ramp and head for Petaluma to be with his wife. That's what Jason had told him to do. He should listen to the experts. They knew how to do this and survive. Then a terrifying image of Carmen and Armando, trapped and helpless, filled his thoughts He approached the southbound on-ramp that would take him toward Petaluma.

He took the ramp heading the other way.

Luis couldn't go. Not yet. He couldn't flee to safety while his loved ones were still in danger. He had to go back and help the firemen whether they wanted him there or not. It was his family and his responsibility.

The smoke was heavy over the freeway, severely limiting his visibility and forcing him to drive slower than he wanted. He grew increasingly agitated as every second ticking away became a lost opportunity to help. If Monica's parents were still alive, they couldn't afford for him to waste time getting to them. He cursed himself for having left in the first place. He should have stayed right there regardless of what the firefighters said. *Well, they won't stop me this time.*

**2:30 a.m.**

Luis was driving back into the heart of the fire. He could see it ahead of him, and it scared him, but he had to keep going. He drove as fast as he could, chafing at the time it was taking him. The smoke was thick, like fog.

Headlights emerged from the smoke, moving toward him. He slowed. *They have to be on the other side of the highway,* he thought, but as more and more headlights came into view through the smoke and the haze, he realized they weren't passing him. They were bearing down on him. They were moving slowly, and as the cars came into full view, they began flashing their lights at him. Luis slowed and came to a stop. One of the cars pulled away from the others and drove up to the Explorer.

A man leaned out the window and shouted. "You can't get through! They closed the freeway ahead! The other side is already completely shut down. You have to turn around!"

The way back to the house was blocked. Luis knew he couldn't find his way using just backroads, and if he tried, he was sure most of them would be blocked by fire or emergency vehicles.

It was over.

He was done.

It was time to go to Petaluma.

Tears stinging his eyes, Luis made a U-turn and joined the caravan of cars driving southbound down the wrong side of the freeway.

# Monica 2:30 a.m.

My body shook as the fire continued to chase us down the freeway. I could hear explosions not far away, but I couldn't see what was exploding or where. The speed and fury of the flames as they raced along the sides of the freeway were astonishing. The lane in front of me cleared for a moment, and I pressed hard on the gas.

The other drivers around us didn't understand. They hadn't seen what we had. They didn't realize this monster was coming for them, to kill them. I screamed at them to drive faster or move out of my way. My hands and arms ached from gripping the steering wheel. I had to be ready when the fire pulled its next trick. I'd watched it fly over the freeway and ignite the other side. What else could it do? What could stop it? Our only chance to survive was for me to be ready to evade at a moment's notice. I couldn't afford to relax.

"Are we almost there?" Arielle asked from the backseat.

Those words struck me deeply. I'd heard Arielle ask that question so many times as a little girl on long drives that it had become routine and a prompt for humor. Coming from her now, it seemed the most important question in the world.

"I hope so." It was the most sincerely I had ever answered my daughter in her entire life.

The truth was I had no idea how close we were. I only knew we were heading in the right direction because the GPS on my phone told me so. My consciousness felt under assault, and I had stopped thinking about time—how much had passed, how much was left. I was just trying to survive the immediate moment, responding to what was right in front of me, a freeway surrounded by a firestorm.

*What if I run out of fuel before the fire does?* I looked down at the gas gauge for the first time since we'd left Dan's house. I was relieved to see we had more than enough gas left to get us where we needed to be.

As long as fire didn't block our path.

According to the map on my phone, we were getting close, but I was too exhausted to take in more than that. I considered handing my phone to Arielle, so she could help me navigate, but I couldn't relinquish being in control. What if we missed the exit because her attention went elsewhere? But what if we missed the exit because I was trying to do too much? Then I realized she was asking me for directions from the backseat rather than look them up on her phone. The GPS was safer with me.

Another explosion rattled the car. I wondered if we would even be safe in Petaluma. Was it burning down, too? How far would we have to run? I glanced to the right and the left. The fire was still chasing us. I took my left hand from the wheel just quickly enough to wipe the sweat and tears from my cheeks before wrapping it tightly around the steering wheel again. I tried not to fixate on my bare ring finger.

**3:30 a.m.**

The minute I pulled up to Joel and Shannon's house, I put the car in park and began crying. My tears were a mixture of relief and grief. I was relieved Arielle and I were safe, that we had reached a place not being threatened by fire. I could still smell the fire, but I couldn't see it, and that in itself gave me a sense of relief I hadn't felt since going to bed hours before. But the grief, confusion, and terror at not knowing where my parents and Luis were occupied nearly all my thoughts

The front door flew open, and Joel and Shannon rushed out. I could see the fear and concern on their faces. They wrapped me in their arms with fierce hugs as I stumbled out of the car. I was still shaking.

"My parents are still up there, and Luis is trying to find them. I haven't heard anything else," I said, then I broke down into choking sobs. "I'm sorry I didn't call first. I . . . I'm just . . ." I didn't even know what I was trying to say.

"It's okay," Shannon said. "We've been debating calling you for hours, but we didn't know what to do."

"Please, please come inside," Joel said.

Arielle got out of the car, wrapped the towel tightly around herself, and put her arms around me from behind. The four of us clung together for a moment, trying to make sense of what was happening. After a minute, Shannon broke free, looked at Arielle, and said, "I've got some clothes you can wear." Then she turned to me, blinked back tears, and said, "Whatever you need, whatever we have, just let me know." Shannon turned back to Arielle and wrapped her arm around her shoulders. "Come inside," she said. Arielle nodded and let Shannon lead her into the house.

Joel and I followed behind. "I'm sure they'll be fine," he said.

I knew he was saying the only thing he could think of given the circumstances, but I had to fight the urge to scream *How do you know they'll be fine!* at the top of my lungs.

Nothing was fine. My parents weren't fine. Luis wasn't fine. Arielle and I weren't fine. I wasn't sure anything was ever going to be fine again. Joel and Shannon hadn't seen what I had seen driving on that mountain and down the freeway. They couldn't comprehend the strength, the anger, and viciousness of this thing Luis and my parents would have to fight. I knew Joel meant well, but he was offering me hope when I needed something more. I needed to know where my family was. I needed to know my parents were together. I needed to know Luis was not out there alone.

Joel turned on the television so that we could watch live news coverage of the fires. Streets we had driven on less than an hour ago were now impassable infernos. I tried to speak but couldn't. I felt nauseous watching the reporters naming the street closures and fire department officials being interviewed and describing how expansive and dangerous this fire was and how quickly it was spreading. I was also shocked to learn there were actually three fires burning out of control through that night, and fire departments had already changed their mission from fighting the fires to performing evacuations and rescues. They acknowledged what I already knew; this was one of the most destructive fires they'd ever seen.

I couldn't help but wonder how Luis would ever make it out of there.

". . . starting mandatory evacuations," a reporter was saying. "The fire is driven by winds that were gusting at almost sixty miles per hour, that's near hurricane-force winds driving the fire. Some areas near Mark West Springs Road are experiencing torna-do-like wind conditions. We've had reports that embers are flying a mile or so ahead of the blaze. And we can now confirm the fires have reached Santa Rosa."

"That was two and a half hours ago!" I spat. "Give me something new. Give me some information I don't already have."

"We are told that evacuation shelters will be opened, and we hope to have a list of those for you shortly. So, please stay tuned. For those who are just joining us, it looks like fire personnel is asking people to evacuate the following neighborhoods . . ."

I had to walk away from the television. I couldn't take this. I tried calling my mom again. It went straight to voicemail. The phone was gone. It had to be. My finger hovered over Luis's name. I desperately wanted to call him, but I was afraid I might distract him at a crucial moment. Worse, I was afraid of what I might learn.

Shannon came into the room with some coffee for me. "How are you holding up?" she asked.

"I feel like I'm about to either explode or completely meltdown."

She looked compassionately at me and took my hand in hers. She didn't say anything.

After a moment, I continued, "I don't know what I'm going to do if I've lost them."

I took a deep breath, felt a hitch in my throat, gulped, and was about to go on, but then Shannon said, "If anyone can get out of there, they can. They're fighters, all of them. Half the stories I've heard about your parents . . ." she trailed off. "Luis will find them."

"I'm worried he will, and then they'll all be trapped." The sting of tears returned. "Oh my God, this is a nightmare. How is this real? How is any of this happening?" I glanced down at my hands. They were clenched into fists. What did I hope to do? I focused on my bare ring finger. In my mind, I saw it resting on the bathroom counter where I'd left it before going to bed. Now it was gone. Luis had given it to me, and it was gone. A kind of panic rose in my chest. Luis had given me a beautiful new life, and he was gone. My parents gave me everything, and now they were gone. What was I going to do with these clenched fists?

I released my hands and crumpled against Shannon's chest and started crying again.

As each minute ticked away, it became harder for me to hope that any of them were still alive. The local news was airing images from the fires, and I couldn't stop watching the screen. I was simultaneously fascinated and repulsed, scanning the news for any clues regarding the whereabouts of my parents and Luis. I found none. The longer I watched, the harder it was to convince myself my loved ones were alive.

"Thank you, Shannon. I don't know what I would have done if we couldn't be here."

Shannon nodded, and I could tell she was on the verge of losing it, too.

"I'm sure . . ." Shannon said, voice cracking slightly. "I mean, I only just met your mom. She's so put together and graceful. And she's funny too." She paused a moment, thinking of what else she could say, then found it: "When we were playing cards, I had this image of her at a baccarat table in Monte Carlo, playing against Dukes and Earls and cleaning them out."

Somehow that image struck me as funny but also true, and I laughed. I could easily picture my mom playing with the rich and famous and refusing to let any of them win. "That's my mom. Dad says she's always been like that. You're right. She's a fighter. Every Caldentey woman is."

"Luis fought for you," Shannon said, her eyes welling up behind her gentle smile. "Just like your dad fought for your mom. The four of you are strong people and blessed to have each other."

"I know," I said. All of this was true, but I was struggling against a sinking sensation that everyone I loved was gone. Drowning there on Shannon's couch, I told myself I had every reason to hope, but dark shadows whispered the opposite. The truth was, I had no idea what had happened to my parents nor why the Chrysler was suddenly no longer behind me. I could only hope they weren't far behind and that Luis found them quickly after Arielle and I kept going.

AFTER ARIELLE AND I KEPT GOING

IT'S BEEN TWO YEARS SINCE THAT DAY. I'M AT THE KITCHEN table of our home in Moss Landing, and I am keenly aware of my reluctance to use the words *after Arielle and I left*.

Two years later, I still struggle with that description, dancing cautiously around the words I use to describe that specific moment because of the implications of writing the truth: *I left my parents and continued down the hill to safety.*

I left my parents—and what?

I left my husband—and what?

Those questions have haunted me ever since.

# Armando y Carmen 3:15 a.m.

*Marilyn Ress, age 71, former nursing assistant, easily recognized around town by her bright red walker and pink cardigans, dies while sleeping in her home on Mendocino Avenue at Journey's End mobile home park.*

WHEN HE CAME UP FOR AIR, ARMANDO'S LUNGS BURNED like they were on fire. A moment later, he heard Carmen gasping beside him.

"Please tell me this will end soon," she whispered. Her voice was raspy.

"Soon there won't be anything left to burn," he promised.

Impossible as it seemed, the fire still raged around them, but he couldn't figure out what was fueling it. The house and everything in the backyard had burnt to the ground. Despite that, debris continued to rain from above. Flames burned so close to the pool he could feel the heat on his face.

An ember landed on Armando's hand. He felt no pain but patted it out anyway. Carmen leaned against his shoulder. She was quietly praying.

"At least we're together," she said.

"*Siempre.*"

The heat from the fire had increased in intensity, and he knew they needed to go back under the water. He worried, though. Carmen's breathing was labored. He knew his was, too, but she seemed to have it worse than he did.

"Are you okay?" Armando asked.

Carmen nodded.

Armando gave his wife a tap on her shoulder, signaling her to go under with him.

They inhaled and plunged back underneath the water. Armando saw Carmen's face before him in the dark, murky water, her hair fanning out like a halo around her head. She smiled at him, and the water combined with her smile reminded him of another time she had smiled at him on a beach in Cuba, as the water lapped at their toes.

They were strolling along, the water splashing Carmen's feet, making her squeal. A few yards behind, one of her maiden aunts, an older, dour woman, trailed behind them. Armando found it intolerable to have her listening to every word he wanted to say to Carmen, and he had some important ones he needed to share.

"Want to escape?" he whispered.

She nodded.

Armando grabbed Carmen's hand, and a moment later, they were running down the beach as fast as they could. The chaperone was shouting, but Armando ignored her. Ahead of them, there was a stand of trees, and he steered them toward it. They finally ducked out of sight, and he turned to look at the girl he loved.

Carmen's cheeks were flushed. Her eyes sparkled. Her lips were parted slightly. Armando stared at her longingly for a moment then took a deep breath.

"My parents are sending me away to a military school in the United States."

Carmen's lips began to tremble, and she shook her head vigorously.

"I know what they're trying to do, and it won't work," he said earnestly. "I will write you every day, and as soon as I finish school, we'll be married."

She bit her lip. Tears shimmered in her eyes.

"You believe me, right?"

She nodded and then looked down at the ground.

"Stay here with me," she said softly.

"You know I can't. But I'll be back."

Armando took a small knife out of his pocket, turned, and carved their initials into one of the trees, putting a heart around it. Finished, he put the knife back. He could hear shouting; several people were looking for them now. They didn't have much time.

Armando looked into Carmen's eyes. *"Te quiero,"* he told her.

*"Te quiero,"* Carmen whispered back, much to his relief.

Their pursuers were very close now. Armando stepped forward and kissed her. Carmen threw her arms around his neck and kissed him back. He could taste salt on her lips. It tasted like tears, and he didn't know if they were hers or his.

At last, Armando pulled away. "I promise you we'll be together," he vowed.

Carmen nodded as her aunt appeared and laid hold of her. The woman shouted at Armando, things a lady should not have said. It was worth it, though. He finally knew that Carmen felt the same way about him as he did about her.

**3:30 a.m.**

Even with the fire burning all around them and layers of smoke rolling over them, Carmen was cold. The water in the pool was cold. The combination of the cold and the burns on her skin broke down her body's defenses from two extremes, each feeding off the other in a way that made her skin and muscles throb in confusion and pain. She wished the cold water would soothe the sting of the burns, but the cold didn't soothe so much as it burrowed into her damaged flesh and sought purchase in the wounds. She shivered uncontrollably, trying her best to hold tightly to Armando. He wished he could do more to keep her warm.

"How long do you think it's been?" She gasped as she spoke.

"Maybe two hours," he said.

"So long." Her teeth chattered.

"We've waited longer. Help should come soon."

"If they made it."

She was the first to voice what they both feared.

Armando began to wonder if his family were safe, and how safe. What if they weren't? What if they were trapped, like he and Carmen were, or worse? What could be worse? He could not stand to imagine worse. He must focus on what he knew and let God manage everything else.

He looked back at Carmen. Her eyes were squeezed shut. Her teeth were chattering. "They made it," he said to her. "Have faith." When he spoke, his teeth chattered, too.

Carmen opened her eyes and looked back at him. The only light was from the fires around them. He hoped she believed their family was safe. It would make surviving the night easier. She closed her eyes again, and he knew she was praying. He prayed, too. He prayed for Monica, Arielle, and Luis. He prayed they had found their way off the burning hill. He prayed they had found help and were waiting somewhere safe. He prayed someone was coming to rescue them.

If it's not too late.

Carmen opened her eyes again and spoke haltingly, coughing as she did. "It's been more than two hours," she said.

"I know," he said. "It doesn't stop. I have no idea why. There's nothing left to burn."

Armando knew Carmen would detect the despair in his words, no matter how hard he tried to conceal it. He changed the subject.

"Do you remember the day I left for Manlius?"

Carmen nodded.

Of course she did. At the age of fourteen, Armando's parents worried he would join the Batista rebels and sent him to military school in the US. Armando was deeply in love, and they feared he and Carmen were too serious. They worried about the possibility of a pregnancy and the shame it would bring to the family. They thought military school would doom the love affair, and that was a perfectly fine secondary outcome as far as they were concerned.

She had stood on the tarmac the day Armando left. The sun beat down on her. In her hands, she clutched a bouquet of white flowers he had given her just before he'd been hauled up the stairs of a nearby plane. At the top of the stairs, in front of the plane door, he turned to her and shouted, "I will write to you every day, Carmen! And I'll come back for you!"

Armando saw Carmen's mother surge forward at his words, but her father didn't move. Carmen told him later that her father had clamped his hand on her shoulder and said sternly, "Let him go." She told Armando she watched him disappear into the plane and knew she would never let him go.

"That was the saddest moment of my life," he said. "I really wasn't sure what would happen next. I just knew what I didn't want to happen."

Carmen clutched his arm. "I will never let you go," she murmured.

"You never did," Armando whispered. "Thank you."

When they were separated, Armando had written Carmen a letter every single day. She wrote back almost as frequently, though it was often difficult because of the busy schedule her parents devised for her. They were equally determined to keep her away from him.

It had been far too long since he'd written his wife a love letter like he used to when they were young. She deserved one. She deserved hundreds, if not thousands by now. He started composing one in his mind. He desperately wanted to share it with her that moment, but they needed to conserve their oxygen and inhale as little smoke as possible. He looked at her. Her face was pale and pinched. She wasn't getting enough oxygen, or she was inhaling too much smoke. Probably both. Still, she was the most beautiful woman he'd ever seen.

### 4:00 a.m.

Armando was exhausted. More than once that night, he felt himself drift off. He snapped awake each time, terrified. Carmen's breathing had become increasingly labored, and like him, she fought to stay conscious against the limited amount of oxygen. She clung to him to help her stay above water. She needed him. If he lost consciousness, they would both die. He couldn't let that happen.

They spoke little. Speaking required breathing, and the only available air was smoke-laden. To stay focused, Armando prayed silently, and he thought about what would happen when they could finally get out of the pool. The rest of the time he spent remembering, reliving every second of their lives together.

He had written to Carmen every day in military school, just as he promised. He was the only sixteen-year-old in his class fixated on marriage, and that made him stand out a bit. He didn't care. He poured his heart and soul into each letter. Carmen wrote back often. She'd tell him about her day, catch him up on the latest news from family and friends, and reassure him that she loved him and was waiting for him. He'd read and reread each of her letters dozens if not hundreds of times. Every letter filled him with joy and longing. Until the day she'd sent him a very different letter.

She wrote that by the time he received the letter, she would likely be in Spain. Carmen was fifteen now, and her parents were taking her there to introduce her to young men they considered appropriate suitors. She gave Armando the address in Spain where she believed they'd be staying and swore she would not look nor talk to a single young man. Armando believed her, but the machinations of her family terrified him. What if her parents forced her into a marriage? How could he find out and stop it in time? He was still in school, and his parents would do nothing to help him get to Spain, particularly if it was in pursuit of Carmen. Armando hastily penned her a letter. He begged her to tell him everything that happened and to keep him informed of anything else her parents did to try and keep them apart.

Carmen spent a year in Spain with her parents, a year that was devastatingly lonely for Armando. Only later did she tell him the full extent of how her parents tried to introduce her to other boys. Carmen had refused to consider any of them, which created a strain in her relationship with her parents that lasted for years. In the end, however, her parents accepted that their daughter would never remove Armando from her heart.

Armando had always assured anyone who might compliment his courage, stability, or strength that whatever portion of those qualities he might exhibit, it was learned from his wife. Carmen was the strongest woman he knew. He had never doubted her strength, and had someone suggested his wife might one day lose her strength or fortitude, he would have laughed and replied, "You don't know my wife."

But now Carmen was weakening. They both were. And Armando worried.

He figured they had been in the pool for two or three hours, moving from one corner to another, back and forth as they tried to keep from being burned or choked to death. The pool was cold and filled with debris and ashes. Acrid smoke hung everywhere. The worst of it was over, he knew that, but it was still obviously too dangerous to get out of the pool. Fire burned everywhere he looked. There was nowhere for them to go. It looked as if the fire had consumed everything that could burn or blow up, but it still refused to die. The pool was their only chance of survival. They just needed to keep moving, keep breathing, and stay awake. Moving around was exhausting. Every muscle in his body cramped uncontrollably. He didn't know how much longer he could keep going.

Whenever the cramps threatened to overwhelm him, and he didn't think he could hold on for another second, Armando would look at his wife. Just one glimpse into her face would give him the strength to keep his grip on the edge of the pool. On the other hand, Carmen's strength was rapidly diminishing; more and more often, she slipped from his shoulder or lost her grip on the pool's edge. He wondered what he would do when she ran out of strength. When the fire had been at its worst, the air quality over the pool had been subject to any number of variables and shifted accordingly. They had moved when the smoke grew too thick or the water too noxious. Now, the air and water quality was still poor but less variable. Still, they moved to stay warm and to stay awake, but they were exhausted, and it was getting harder and harder to move.

Looking at her now, holding her head above the black murk in the pool, she had never looked more beautiful. He was so grateful to have spent his life by her side. This rush of emotion overwhelmed him. Then suddenly, inexplicably, it left him with a strength he hadn't felt in hours. He wrapped his arms under hers and gently guided her to the other side of the pool. They had to keep moving to stay awake, and they needed to stay awake to stay alive.

The pool had lost a lot of water, and the branches and ash dumped into it by the wind and fire made it increasingly hard for Armando and Carmen to get their heads completely submerged. At times, their mouths and noses would be exposed to the air, and a gust of wind would blow the water straight over their faces, pushing sulfurous sludge down their throats and into their nostrils. When this happened, they were forced to surface. They coughed terrible, painful coughs to expel what they had involuntarily swallowed. Where they were now was awful, but at least it provided them a measure of safety. Despite the pain, fear, and exhaustion, he would not give up. He could not give up. If they could just outlast the fire, someone would come for them.

# Luis 4:00 a.m.

LUIS HAD BEEN STUCK IN THE EXODUS OF CARS FLEEING
Santa Rosa for more than an hour, inching along a few feet every
minute. He spent most of his time on the road waiting for the
cars in front of him to move. While he waited, he stared straight
ahead, barely aware of anything outside except his wife, whom he
prayed was waiting for them at Joel and Shannon's. He could call
and check, but that would force him to admit a truth he couldn't
yet admit to himself: he had failed. Luis looked at the world outside the windows of the Explorer: a black night of raging fire and
choking smoke, and hundreds of scared, desperate people seeking to escape.

He leaned his forehead against the wheel and said a prayer for
his in-laws and another for his wife. A car horn blared from his
right. He looked over and saw two adults, a man behind the wheel
and a woman next to him in an aging, battered Toyota. They were
trying to keep him from drifting into their lane. In the backseat,
there was a young boy with a flat face and a short neck looking at
him through the window. The child smiled at him. Luis wanted to
look away, but he forced himself to smile back and wave.

He didn't know how he was going to explain to Monica why Carmen and Armando weren't with him, but there was only so much one could do. The rest was up to God. He shifted in his seat, put his shoulders back, slapped his cheeks lightly, and slowly took his foot off the brake, letting the Explorer roll forward.

# Monica 4:30 a.m.

I HAD BEEN LOOKING OUT THE WINDOW OF JOEL AND Shannon's living room for over an hour, lost in a haze of fear, watching for Luis when I saw the Explorer's headlights turn onto the street. I ran to the car to meet him.

When I reached the driveway, Luis was standing outside the SUV. My parents were not in the cab.

Luis was alone.

He looked up at me, devastated. I threw my arms around him, and he pulled me in tightly.

"I tried. I really did," Luis said. "I made it almost all the way back up there, but there was a tree down, and I couldn't pass it. The firemen ordered me to evacuate. I gave one of them my phone number, and he promised me he'd get up there and that he'd call if he found them."

"Did you find their car?" I asked.

"No, but I couldn't see much," he admitted.

"Maybe they made it down, and we didn't see them? Or maybe the firefighters didn't."

"I hope so," he said.

I pulled away from him. "They've announced where the evacuation centers are, let's go check them out. If they made it down, maybe someone directed them there." He nodded and followed me into the house.

Joel and Shannon were waiting for him at the front door, and they embraced him immediately. "This is awful," Shannon whispered. "I don't even know what to say, but please tell me what we can do."

"Anything you need, just tell us," Joel added.

Luis nodded. I was staring at the television, watching people being escorted into evacuation shelters. "Let's go," I said, heading toward the door.

"Do you need us to go with you?" Joel asked.

I shook my head. "Just take care of Arielle and call us if you hear anything."

"We will," Shannon said. Then she added, "Be safe, please."

Moments later, we were in the car. I sat in the passenger seat, overwhelmed by the relief at having Luis next to me, and the grief that we still didn't know where my parents were. I hoped we'd find something that would kill the ugly fear that had begun gnawing at my insides.


I WANTED TO SCREAM AS WE WOUND THROUGH THE CLOGGED streets trying to get to the first evacuation shelter: a church in Petaluma. The shelters were set up in churches, schools, and fairgrounds and scattered from Petaluma up to Monte Rio and Guerneville, over thirty miles northwest of us, an impossible drive given traffic and fire conditions. There was no way we could make it to all of them, but we would get to as many as we could. We took detour after detour down side streets, running into one roadblock after another. In the darkness of some of the smaller roads, we couldn't see the barriers until we almost crashed into them.

At this point, my moods swung between desperation and anger. After we'd been driving around Petaluma for what seemed like forever, I shouted, "This is insane! What good is an emergency shelter if no one can get to it?" Luis didn't say anything, but he squeezed my hand for a moment before putting his own back on the steering wheel. I was glad he was driving. I wished he'd been driving when we left the house, but I couldn't waste my energy thinking about that, though. I had to focus on the here and now.

We turned into a parking lot. "This is it," he announced, his voice tight.

I was out of the car as soon as it stopped. The parking lot was full of people huddled in vehicles, trying to sleep. Others just stood beside them, crying and hugging each other. As we neared the building, I saw people on the ground, curled up, some with blankets, but many, perhaps most, without anything but the clothes they were wearing, and almost everyone was wearing pajamas or sweats. Some seemed dazed, shellshocked. They sat on the ground or leaned against cars. They stood in mute silence with unfocused eyes, while others cried and paced or rocked back and forth on the ground, their arms clutching their knees to their chests. Parents held children protectively in their arms. I was surprised by the number of dogs, but glad to see them with their owners.

When we got inside, we discovered why so many people were in the parking lot. It was nearly impossible to walk around the bedraggled mass of people sitting and lying on the ground. Children were crying, dogs were barking, and the combined noise was deafening. I was stunned and heartbroken by the collective misery in the room and wondered where to start looking.

"How do we do this?" Luis asked.

"Maybe they've started a missing persons list that we can put their names on."

"Or maybe there's a list of people that are here."

I nodded, then suggested we split up and try to find someone in charge. I didn't want to leave Luis's side, but navigating our way through the building, let alone successfully finding anyone among the chaotic mass, would go faster this way, and I knew time was slipping away from us.

He agreed and took off toward the other side of the room.

I turned and began picking my way through the crowd, looking for a sign of my dad's pajamas or my mom's clothes. There were too many people, though, draped in blankets or wearing coats and sweatshirts. So, focusing on clothes, I started looking at faces. I looked at every single person I could, into one face after another, and as I did, I could see my desperation reflected in theirs.

Some embraced friends and family, while others embraced strangers. Small clusters of people prayed together, some silently and some out loud. The young, old, rich, and poor were all gathered here, united in loss and suffering. Children gathered around the dogs, petting and hugging them, and the dogs were quick to lick the children's faces in return.

The entire scene was tragic and yet hopeful, and I struggled with my response to it, veering between compassion and empathy for all of these strangers, and anger and frustration at being alone in their midst, looking for my parents.

I saw volunteers setting up giant urns of coffee and rows of paper cups on a long table against a wall and off to the side. I headed over. If my mom were here, she'd probably be trying to volunteer and help others.

This was the first positive thought I'd had in hours.

I reached the table. "Excuse me, is there a missing persons list?"

The woman closest to me shook her head. "I don't know, but the director would." She pointed to a man on the other side of the room.

I headed straight for him, reaching him at the same time Luis did. Luis looked at me and shook his head. There was no sign of my parents.

"Excuse me, we're looking for my parents," I said. "Have you started a missing persons list?"

The man passed a weary hand over his face. "No, not yet. We should do that. Give me a minute."

He shuffled off quickly.

"I'm going to finish looking over there," Luis said, waving toward the back.

"Okay."

He headed off, and every few feet, I could hear him shouting, "Armando! Carmen!"

I shifted my weight anxiously back and forth while I waited for the director to return.

He came back a few minutes later with a yellow legal pad and a pen. I snatched it from his hands and wrote down my parents' names, followed by my name and phone number to call if they were located. I stared for a moment at the list I had just started. *How many others like my parents were still missing?*

Tears welled up in my eyes, and I handed it back to the man, feeling more helpless than hopeful. I couldn't just rely on someone else to find them and then maybe check this list and eventually get around to calling me. Suddenly the entire idea seemed futile and stupid.

I took a deep breath and reminded myself my parents would call me as soon as they were able. My mom, at least, would know my cell number from memory. She would call. If they were still alive, she would have called.

She hadn't called.

A strangled scream of frustration escaped my lips. The director looked at me with compassion in his tired eyes.

"I'm sorry," he said.

"Thank you. Thank you for what you're doing," I said, then I turned and walked away, looking for Luis and wondering how many times the director would say those words before he got some sleep.

As I walked toward Luis, I looked around the room. There was so much grief and loss etched into the faces around me. I saw a place packed with strangers, but walking among them, I detected something I hadn't expected: a sense of love and compassion in the face of shared hardship. Strangers were treating each other like family.

I reached Luis and stood by his side, mute, taking all of this in.

"They're not here," he said, voice resigned. "I have some people looking out for them, though."

I took a deep breath. "Let's go to the next one."

By the time we made it out to the parking lot, there were even more people arriving, some by car, others on foot. I watched seven or eight people fall out of a small, compact car. It was like watching clowns at the circus. The look on their faces, though, was anything but comical. They were tired, frightened, and dazed, and they staggered as they got out and walked around the car.

I had to turn away, wishing again my parents had just gotten into my car instead of trying to take theirs. Moments later, as Luis slowly steered the Audi out of the parking lot, I caught a glimpse of the bedraggled group limping toward the building. My heart went out to them, and I couldn't help but wonder if they managed to get everyone they needed to into that tiny car.

I glanced at the time. It was almost half-past six in the morning. It had taken us nearly two hours just to get here and search this one shelter. At least the others weren't too far away.

Luis turned on the radio so we could listen to the news.

"More areas of Santa Rosa are being evacuated as the firestorm continues its charge. Firefighters are urging anyone in the affected areas or nearby to evacuate to safety. Do so immediately to avoid being trapped by the fire when it gets too close. It is moving at a fearsome speed and anyone who delays evacuating risks perishing. Again, this fire has exceeded everyone's expectations, and it looks like things are about to get a whole lot worse."

"It's hard to imagine worse," Luis muttered.

I thought of the way the embers had flown straight at the car, pelting the windshield. It had been like rain in a storm. A firestorm.

"It's a firestorm," I said. "How do you stop a storm?"

"I don't know."

We had to drive around several more roadblocks. Some of the streets were eerily desolate, and others showed signs of people fleeing the fires. The sky grew light, and the horizon in every direction glowed red. It wasn't the sun rising; it was the fire burning. It looked like the end of the world.

Maybe it is, I thought.

# Armando y Carmen 4:30 a.m.

*Valerie Evans, age 75, an animal lover known to neighbors as "the horse lady" whose property also housed goats, a mule, and a donkey, dies at her home in Santa Rosa while trying to save her dogs. According to a neighbor who tried to help her, she shooed him away, saying, "We got this."*

"Talk to me."

Armando shifted slightly. He was having trouble breathing, and his chest burned from all the smoke he'd inhaled. He knew it was worse for Carmen. The fire still raged everywhere, and the smoke was so thick it made them gag and choke. Both of them were shivering, but Carmen could barely breathe.

"I'm here," he said.

"My chest hurts."

"Mine too, *mi amor*."

"You looked so handsome when we got married," his wife said softly, her eyes glassy.

"Not half as handsome as you were beautiful. No one has ever seen such a bride."

Armando pulled Carmen closer to him. She put her face to his chest and coughed violently against his skin.

"I can't feel my fingers," she said. Armando could tell from the way her hands held his arms that her grip was weakening.

Her body trembled against his. "How much longer until we can get out?" Carmen asked. "I'm so cold."

Armando looked around. There was nothing left of Dan's house, but the fire still burned across the canyon and up the mountainside. It seemed impossible there was anything left to burn, but the fire raged on, creating endless clouds of smoke they couldn't escape while the wind blew ash and embers everywhere.

"Close your eyes," Armando told her.

Carmen whispered, "When we are out of this, I want to sleep in our bed for a week."

"Me too," he said. "How are your burns?"

"Everything is numb, or it hurts. I can't tell the difference. . . . Warm and dry. . . . In our bed."

Carmen opened her mouth, and Armando waited for her next words. Instead, she coughed violently. He held her in his arms while her body shuddered under the black water. Her limbs spasmed, and she unintentionally kicked his shin. Armando put his cheek as close to Carmen's as he dared. He was careful not to make contact because of his burns.

"Monica and Luis," she said.

"I don't know."

"Mandi . . . I . . ."

Armando waited, but Carmen didn't say anything else. He could hear her wheezing.

After so many years together, they had become, in a genuine sense, a single being. Most of the time, Armando could sense Carmen's thoughts, desires, and needs long before she had a chance to express them. Someone had once commented on this aspect of their relationship as evidence of the intensity of their love. His daughter Monica had disagreed. "It isn't the intensity of their love that makes them special," Monica had said. "It's that my parents make loving another person look easy, that it is the most natural, desirable thing in the entire world." *Perhaps,* Armando thought. *But it was easy to love Carmen.*

"It's okay. The worst has to be over. We just need to hold on a little longer," he said.

Armando pulled his cheek from Carmen's and looked in her eyes.

"Stay here with me," he said.

**4:45 a.m.**

Armando was worried. The water temperature was dangerously cold. He and Carmen shook uncontrollably. The fire was finally dying around them, but it still didn't feel safe leaving the pool. He kept them moving around in search of less toxic air, but the pool measured twenty by forty feet, and they could only go so far. Armando also moved to keep the blood circulating. He needed to keep them as warm as he could. The water was so full of debris that moving became a challenge. Carmen's grip on him had weakened to the point he had to hold her up with his arms, suspending her body between his and the edge of the pool.

Armando knew from his wife's labored breathing that she was in pain and having trouble. Her lungs weren't as strong as his, and he worried they would give out on her. He didn't know what he could do about that except try to keep moving to areas where there was less smoke. The air around them was still smokey, and ash fell steadily over everything, but occasional gusts of wind created clear pockets for a minute or two, giving them a slight respite from the assault on their lungs.

His wife didn't say anything else. Carmen seemed to have lost her voice, so to keep her attention, Armando said little prayers out loud for both of them until a coughing fit would force him to stop. As he prayed, he looked into her eyes to maintain their connection. She smiled weakly and kept her eyes closed, but he knew she was praying along with him.

As the flames lessened, Armando thought about what came next. How would they make their way to safety? Would Monica and Luis be waiting for them, or had they died in the blaze? It was a terrifyingly real possibility. He knew they would have had to drive straight through the fire down a long, steep, winding canyon road to escape. Armando murmured a prayer for them and their safety. His wife nodded her head gently in agreement and rested it on his shoulder. He held her tighter, wishing he could give her the warmth she needed, but there was no warmth left in his body to give. Still, he clung to her, willing her to live. The roar of the fire and wind had diminished just enough so that he could hear a frightening wheeze every time she exhaled.

For their entire life together, Armando had been Carmen's protector, and he loved the role. Now he felt helpless, an excruciating thing for him to accept. Armando had never let his wife down. If he were alone and stranded in this pool by himself, he could have coped with that, as long as Carmen was safe. Undergoing this ordeal with her, worrying for her safety, witnessing her struggle and her pain was almost too much.

"*Te quiero,*" he whispered.

Carmen nodded. It was the only way she could say it back. It was enough. He'd heard the words from her thousands of times, and he was determined to hear them thousands more.

"Just a little bit longer," Armando said softly.

**5:00 a.m.**

Carmen stirred in Armando's arms. He was aware it had been some time since she'd spoken out loud. She drifted off somewhere for just a few seconds, then fluttered her eyes. For a moment, he thought she was leaving him. He didn't want to ask her any questions. He didn't want to do anything that would steal what little strength she had left, but he wanted to talk with her at this moment more than he ever had in his entire life.

Armando tried to imagine what she was thinking and feeling. Did Carmen know her time was coming to an end? If so, what did she want him to know? What would she want him to remember? What could he do for her?

If Carmen's time were coming to an end, Armando imagined she would be remembering the faces of beloved family members long gone. She would see them smiling at her, greeting her, and holding out their arms to her. She would recall the sounds of their voices and hear the echoes of their laughter. He remembered this had happened with her mother when she passed away.

Armando knew his wife would be thinking about their family: Monica, Carmen Teresa, and Armando, Jr. And the grandchildren and the great-grandchildren to come. She would be thinking of all the joys of life she had yet to share with them: games to play and events to celebrate, graduations, weddings, baby showers, and birthdays. She would be thinking of all she had learned from a lifetime of experiences she had yet to share with her family.

Armando knew all this with utter certainty.

He could not imagine living without Carmen. Just weeks before, after returning home from a trip to South America and the Galapagos Islands, he had brought up the subject of death for the first time in their marriage. He knew it would be something she wouldn't want to discuss—surely they had many years ahead of them—but they were in their seventies, and he thought they should at least acknowledge their life together would one day come to an end. He had tried to be lighthearted about it, gently teasing her.

"What will you do after I'm gone, my love?" He asked the question in a singsong way as if reciting romantic verse.

"What? What are you talking about, Mandi?"

"One day, it will be just you. It's a long way off, I know, but one day . . ." he trailed off, still trying to keep his tone light.

"Shhh. Really. Don't talk to me about this." Then Carmen caught his tone, and volleyed back, "Besides, the question you're asking is all wrong. You need to ask yourself 'What will *you* do without *me*?'"

He laughed, shrugged his shoulders, and said, "Nothing. What can I do without you?"

"That's right," she said, now smiling. "Who will share your mornings with you? How will you cook? Who will cheer you on, love you, and kiss you goodnight? I obviously can't go anywhere. I'll stay right here, thank you."

Yes, Carmen, stay here with me. Please stay.

Armando's chest and ribcage ached. His muscles were fatigued from lack of oxygen. He looked at his wife's face. He watched her breathe. He knew her pain was worse. Her breathing had turned short and shallow, and sometimes she struggled to inhale at all. He looked for any signs of panic, but she remained calm, despite her apparent physical distress. He had to get them more air.

Armando moved them to the center of the pool to a spot where the wind was blowing the smoke away. He encouraged her to breathe. Carmen tried to inhale deeply, but she coughed so hard her entire body shook, and he feared she might blackout.

"Stay awake. Just a little longer," Armando pleaded. "I need you. We all need you."

They had been nearly twenty-four hours without sleep. For the past five hours, they had moved back and forth through 43-degree water, searching for air they could breathe. The lack of oxygen and exhaustion was pulling them both toward sleep. Armando fought the urge to sleep. He forced his eyes open as wide as he could and caressed Carmen's arms, to provide her with some warmth. Armando gently placed his palm against her cheek, then his lips to her skin. Carmen's eyes opened. The corners of her mouth curled into a faint smile.

**5:15 a.m.**

Armando moved them again, this time to the side of the pool. Carmen was too weak to move on her own, so he held her in his arms.

Carmen had been drifting in and out of consciousness for the past few minutes. Each time Armando worried she was slipping away from him, and he'd panic, then she'd open her eyes, find his, and blink a couple of times, calming him.

He continued to pray out loud. His throat was parched, and each word scratched like sandpaper, but it was the only way he knew to keep her attention. She would nod along as best she could. She appeared to be fighting for him as much as he was fighting for her, but he knew they could only fight so long.

He could never have imagined how relentless and lengthy the fire's assault would be, nor that they would need to spend hours in the pool trying to keep it from devouring them. Hours. He didn't know exactly how many, but that fact seemed incredible to him. If they could just hold out until dawn, it might all be over. Daylight would change everything if they could hold on that long.

## 7:00 a.m.

The fire had finally retreated, leaving them surrounded in the blackness of a smoke-filled night. Another ten or fifteen minutes, and it would be daylight. The sun wouldn't be visible, but it would be daylight. He could see an opportunity to get out of the pool wasn't far off. He still held Carmen in his arms. "Daylight's almost here," he said. The words came out in a scratchy whisper, barely audible. "We'll leave then."

Armando didn't know how long he'd scanned the horizon for the approach of day. When the clouds of smoke hanging over them grew lighter, he knew dawn was approaching, and a sense of relief flooded through his body. It didn't diminish his pain, but it lifted his spirit. Just as his eyes had been turned to the light, he had the sensation his wife was pulling his eyes to her. He turned and smiled at her, just as he had every morning for the past fifty-five years.

Carmen opened her eyes, and Armando started. He had seen every side of his wife in a way that went beyond intimate. He knew every emotion, every expression, every twitch and slight change in her lips. But now, for the first time in all their years together, he saw something he had never seen before.

Carmen was smiling in a way that transcended all the pain Armando knew she must be feeling. Incredibly, a warmth flushed through her skin into his hands and radiated outward, warming his chest. She looked deeply into his eyes as if she wanted to penetrate his soul, to open it up and hold it in her hands. This warmth was followed by a tingling sensation in Armando's limbs, where Carmen's skin touched his.

Then he knew. Carmen was leaving him.

Her lips parted briefly. Armando put his ear to her mouth, desperate to hear what she would say, and heard her last breath against his face.

He pulled away to look back into her eyes, but they were closed. Her lips were closed. Her face was relaxed.

Carmen was in his arms, but she was gone.

Armando pulled her as close to him as he could, holding her body to his with all his remaining strength, and he sobbed into her beautiful hair, now burnt, wasted, and wet. He held onto her, keening into her hair, as her body grew cold again. He shivered, the coldness suddenly unbearable to endure alone. He waited, wondering if God was going to take him, too. That would be okay, he thought, but as the seconds ticked by, he knew he wasn't going with her. It wasn't his time. It could only mean there was more for him to do before he could join her. "I'll join you when I can," he whispered against her cheek and held her there for the last time in the blackened ash-filled water.

The sun rose, casting a strange, hazy light through the smoke. The night was over. Armando linked the new day with the passing of more than just the horror of the night; it was a line of demarcation. He must act, but how? What first? What mattered? It would be the first decision in over sixty years that he would make without Carmen.

It was impossible to think that he had just spent his last night with Carmen. Impossible to believe that the first sparks that ignited the house and the mountainside around them had been little more than the initial vanguard of a vast army of marching fire devils, miles deep, that would advance on them, merciless and unwavering, for nearly seven hours.

Armando might have thought it all an unimaginable nightmare were it not for the weight of his wife's body in his arms. He carried her to the exposed steps of the pool. He placed her body upright, seated on a step, with her shoulder resting against the concrete side. He did this as gently as he could, trying to make her as comfortable as possible, as he would have if she were alive. Gently, he clasped her hands together.

Now came the impossible part. He had to let go. He must leave. If he didn't, he would succumb to the physical and emotional stress of the last few hours. Carmen would not want that for him nor their family. He let out an anguished cry and turned away.

The steps belonged to Carmen now; they were not his to use. He would need to lift himself out. The pool was six feet deep and had lost more than two feet of water. So, with the waterline that far from the edge, it would be difficult to climb out. Armando placed his hands against the side of the pool and pushed. His arms shook, but he brought his torso to the edge before they gave out, and he collapsed onto the concrete apron, his legs still hanging into the pool.

The concrete had retained heat from the fire and was warm. Armando lifted his legs out of the pool one at a time. He was finally out of the water. He rolled onto his back. The warmth felt good. He pressed the palms of his hands against it. It was over. He closed his eyes and lost consciousness.

*Carmen Berriz dies of hypothermia and cardiac arrest in the arms of her husband, Armando. The couple, married for fifty-five years, had spent their lives together since they were children growing up in Cuba. Driving away from the flames, the couple's car became stuck in a flower bed. They fled the car and sought refuge in a nearby swimming pool, where they spent hours waiting for the flames to subside while the fire burned down everything around them.*

# Photographs

First trip to Mallorca, Spain. *(left to right)* Cousin Bartolome Caldentey, Carmen (age 10), mother Carmela, and father Juan, 1951

Carmen, age 15, on the cruise ship headed to Mallorca, and away from Armando, 1957

One of Carmen's "appropriate" suitors seen here at Juan's birthday celebration *(from left to right)*: Maria, Lorenzo, Amparo, Josefa, Magdalena, Micaela, Bartolome, "suitor" (name unknown), Carmen, Antonia, Dolores, Toni, Tolo, Tomeu, Carmela and Juan, Mallorca, 1957

Carmen on her way to school at the American Dominican Academy, Havana, 1958

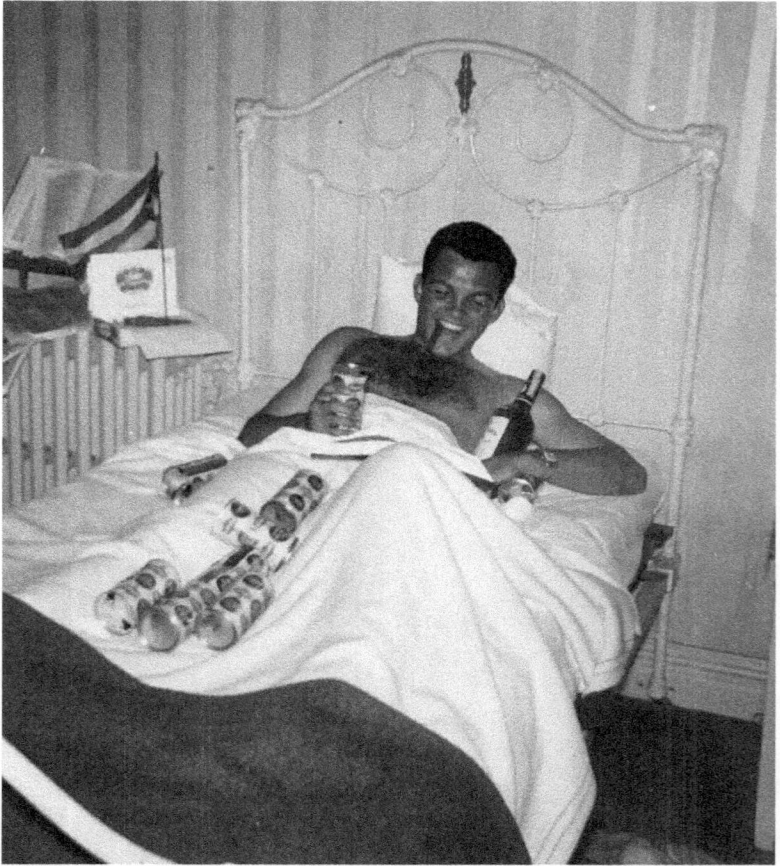

Armando at Villanova University, clowning around, 1957

Carmen and her family arrive in Miami *(from left to right)*: Carmen, her father Juan, her mother Carmela, and her brother Juan, Miami, 1960

The chaperones *(left to right)*: Carmen's brother, Juan Caldentey, and Armando's sister, Bertica Berriz, Armando and Carmen, Key Biscayne, Florida, 1959

The chaperones again *(left to right)*: Juan Caldentey, Armando, Carmen, and Bertica Berriz, 1959

Wedding day *(from left to right)*: Bertica Berriz, Armando, Armando Senior, Berta Berriz, Carmen, Carmela Caldentey, Juan P. Caldentey, Juan Caldentey, Albert Berriz, Miami, Florida, June 1, 1961

Carmen, Wedding day, Miami, Florida, June 1, 1961

Armando and Carmen beginning their 56 years of married life together, June 1, 1961

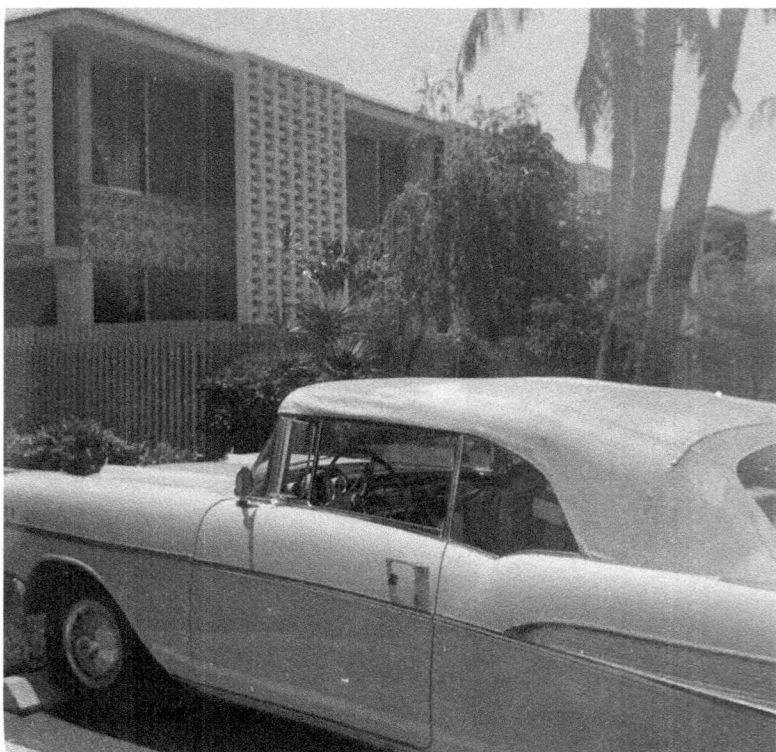

The '57 Chevy Carmen and Armando drove to California, June
1961

50th Wedding anniversary, 2011

Berriz family photo *(left to right)*: Armando A., Monica, Carmen, Armando J., Carmen Teresa, 2009

Carmen, Armando and Juan stopping for tea on the excursion to Tivoli Gardens, Copenhagen, Denmark, July 2015

First trip to Napa Valley, Armando, Carmen, Monica and Luis, Oct 2009

Second trip to Napa, arriving at Dan's house: Carmen, Luis, Monica and Armando, Oct 7, 2017

Dan Brown's house, Santa Rosa, California—front door, Oct 7, 2017

Dan Brown's house, Santa Rosa, California—backyard, Oct 7, 2017

Dan Brown's house, Santa Rosa, California—side yard, Oct 7, 2017

Dan Brown's house, Santa Rosa, California—pool, Oct 7, 2017

Dan Brown's house, Santa Rosa, California—living room, Oct 7, 2017

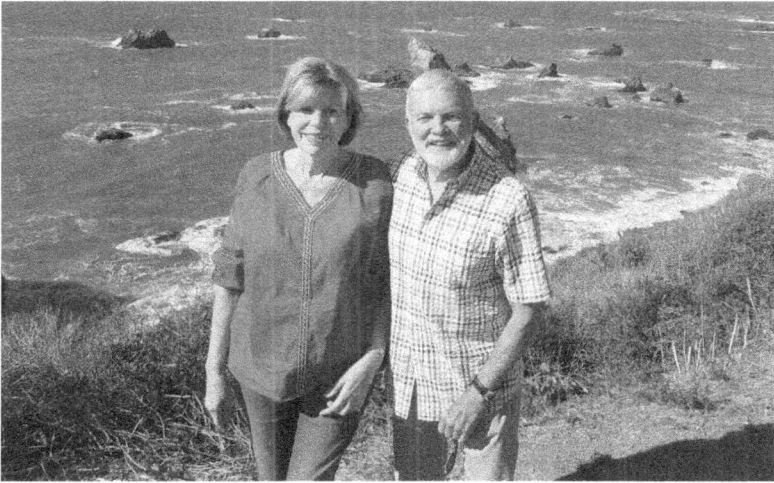

Bodega Bay, Oct 8, 2017

Lunch with the Taatjes *(left to right)*: Shannon, Monica, Luis, Joel, Armando and Carmen, Oct 8, 2017

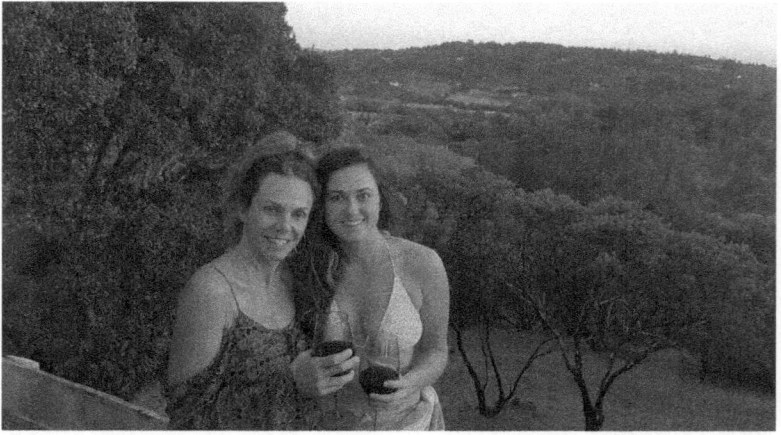

Monica with Arielle poolside at dusk, Oct 8, 2017

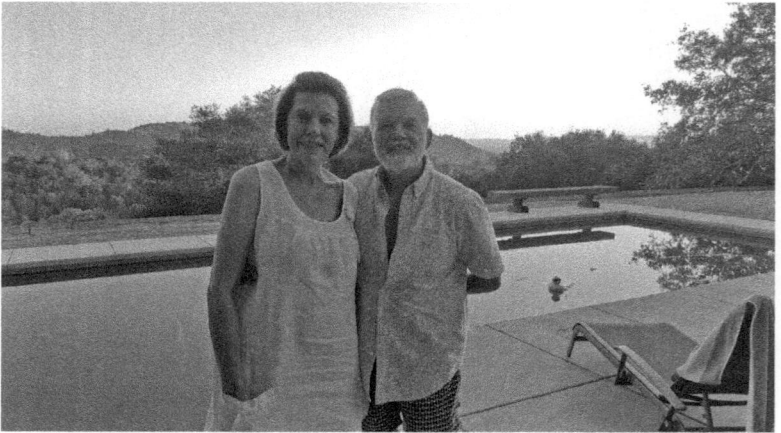

Carmen and Armando photographed together, in front of the pool they would flee to for safety, just hours later, Oct 8, 2017

Last photo of Carmen, playing Sorry, Oct 8, 2017

Dan Brown's house, after the Tubbs fire, Santa Rosa, California—front door, November 2017

Dan Brown's house, after the Tubbs fire—backyard, November 2017

Dan Brown's house, after the Tubbs fire—pool, November 2017

Dan Brown's house, after the Tubbs fire—side yard, November 2017

Armando and Carmen's Chrysler 300, November 2017

The flower bed where the Chrysler
got stuck, November 2017

Luis and Monica look for her wedding ring in the ruins of Dan's
house, November 2017

For the last time in the Apple Valley house, sharing good memories *(from left to right)*: Carmen Teresa, Monica, Luis, Armando, Armando Jr, October 2019

Apple Valley moving crew *(from left to right)*: Kevin Kiesau, Carmen Teresa, Monica, Armando, Luis, Armando Jr, October 2019

Armando appreciating how life is filled with new joys, as he holds his first great grandchild, Brayden, given to him by Arielle and Dennis Zmijewski, Salinas, California, October 2020

# Luis 8:00 a.m.

LUIS COULD TELL MONICA WAS GROWING INCREASINGLY despondent as they arrived at the third shelter, a high school in Santa Rosa. There had been no sign of Armando and Carmen at the second shelter, just more terrified and tired people. She gripped her silent phone as they drove through the endless detours, passing blocked roads and clusters of cars jammed with frustrated, scared drivers, their pets, and belongings. If Armando and Carmen had made it past that fire truck at the bottom of the mountain, they would have already found a way to call them, cell phone or not. But her phone didn't ring, so they kept moving, kept searching, and kept telling themselves there was some kind of miracle waiting for them at the next shelter.

With each breath, Luis swallowed the grief and the guilt of having destroyed their family, and it was suffocating him. *Why didn't I realize sooner they weren't behind me? Why should I be alive if they've perished? Why had I chosen that house?* Monica's silence from the passenger seat echoed his thoughts, only louder and more insistently.

The third shelter was even more packed than the first two, jammed with screaming infants, frightened children and animals, and barely controlled adults in varying stages of shock and grief. The tense press of bodies mashed together made the place hot and stuffy. Once they got their bearings, they searched the room the same way they did the others: find the person in charge, check the list, split up, look at all the faces, call out Armando and Carmen's names.

For Luis, it felt perfunctory. Hope had been supplanted by despair, and its weight pressed against his chest as he searched for two familiar faces among hundreds. "Armando! Carmen!" he shouted. Nothing. He stopped a volunteer. "Have you seen an older couple, Armando and Carmen? He's probably wearing pajamas."

"I'm sorry," the woman said. "There are a lot of people here, though. Do you want me to help you look?"

"No, that's okay," he said, eyeing the mound of blankets in her arms. He didn't want to pull her away from taking care of those with immediate needs so she could help him look for two people who weren't there. He kept moving through the room anyway, calling out their names, asking people if they'd seen them. It took him a few minutes of feeling his wife trailing behind him to realize he hadn't looked her in the eyes since they'd entered the shelter.

So, he turned, looked into her eyes, wrapped his arms around her shoulders, and said quietly into her ear, "They're not here."

They both understood why.

"Call Joel, please, just in case?" she asked him.

Luis called from the middle of that miserable shelter floor.

Joel picked up on the second ring. "Hey, you heard anything?"

"No. We've been to three shelters. There's no sign of them." He sighed. "Have you heard anything?"

"No. Arielle's boyfriend said he was going to drive up, but I think we talked him out of it. I hope we did. I get that she needs him right now, but it's way too risky. He might not even be able to make it here if he tried."

"Thanks. Good call," Luis assured him. The last thing they needed was for Dennis to be lost or stranded with the risk of the fire killing him, too. "How's she doing?"

"Not good. She's pretty freaked out. We all are."

The best thing he could do at this point was to get Monica back to Joel and Shannon's so she could be with Arielle. Splitting them up is what led to this mess.

*That's your fault, too*, said a savage voice in his head.

He turned to Monica, "Arielle's pretty shaken up. We should probably get back there before we can't."

She nodded.

Luis ended the call. "Let's go."

As they headed for the parking lot, Luis kept a step behind Monica. The air between them was heavy with the words they wouldn't say. They climbed into the car. Monica stared down at the phone in her lap.

"I'm going to call my uncle," she said. "I need to hear his voice."

Juan and Andrea were driving down from Oregon. They'd left as soon as they heard about the fire. Luis tried to hear both sides of the conversation, but he couldn't make out what Andrea was saying.

"Yes . . . No, there's no news. . . . I don't know. I just don't know. . . . I'm so scared, Tata, what do we do? . . . If I find them there, what do we ask? . . . Okay . . . Thank you . . . Thank you . . . Yes, I will. We'll see you soon."

"He said we need to check all the hospitals."

Luis was behind the wheel, but his mind was in a hundred different places. At Dan's. At Joel and Shannon's. On Crystal Court. No matter how much he tried to focus on what was right in front of him, his mind kept pulling him back to Crystal Court. The moment he drove through the wall of flame. Watching Monica leave. The look in the fireman's eyes when he told him he had to leave. Sometimes he had to ask himself, *Where are we going? What are we doing next?* Sometimes he had to think for a few seconds before the answer came, which gave him something else to worry about.

Luis looked over at Monica. She stared silently out the passenger side window. Was she watching the morning sun try to push itself out of a haze of smoke and ash? Was she wondering at the sickly, yellow-brown color of the sky? Just looking at it made him cough. He didn't even want to know what toxic particulates they were breathing in.

The silence which had landed between them at the last shelter sat like an immovable boulder between them. Luis desperately wanted to break it but wasn't sure how. Much to his surprise, she beat him to it.

"So, what do you think? Lead and asbestos on top of the woodsmoke? Who knows what toxic crap we're breathing in right now." Monica stared out the window at a group of people hurrying down the street. They were wearing masks. By now, most everyone on the streets, inside the shelters, and at the hospital was wearing masks. They didn't have any. He didn't even think to ask for one. Another failure.

The pessimism and anger in her voice took him aback. She hardly ever spoke this way. It was so unexpected that it took him a moment to thread the needle.

"I think it's going to be okay. Maybe hard, but okay." That was all he could offer.

"I hope so," she said very softly. Then she added, "I'm sorry."

"It's okay. I am too."

Monica took his hand and squeezed it, then she turned her face away and looked out the window. Luis knew she was crying. He gulped, fighting back tears.

Driving in the dark had been unnerving and exhausting, and during the night, he'd kept wishing it were daylight. Not only would it be easier to see what was happening around him, but he wanted to believe it would diminish the scope of horror gnawing at him. Now here was daylight. He could actually see everything around them, and it made everything worse. Nothing was hidden, including the darkest thoughts and the dread he'd hoped would never see the light.

Luis felt as if he were driving in circles as they struggled to make their way to the freeway. The GPS wasn't able to keep up with everything happening in real-time, so they'd stopped believing what it showed, then abandoned even checking it. Every other street seemed to be blocked by police cars parked with their lights flashing, fire engines with crews at work, or burning buildings. He finally found a line of vehicles moving in the same direction, away from the chaos.

"Let's hope they know where they're going," he muttered as he joined them.

A few minutes later, they turned onto a jammed coastal road. Everyone was fleeing the fire, taking the most remote route possible, and it was the worst traffic they'd experienced yet. Luis drove them forward in a crawl, riding the bumper of the car in front of them.

"This is insane," Monica said.

"I know," he agreed. *I know*. It wasn't saying much, but it was all he had, and he needed to acknowledge Monica's voice, to let her know he was listening and present. Besides, she was right. It *was* insane. They both knew how fast fire could burn alongside a road, and he didn't want to be trapped if it made its way here. He looked for an exit. Nothing. They were stuck following the cars in front of them until they could find a way back to the freeway. Out of habit, Monica checked the GPS looking for some sign that things might improve up ahead.

She said, "According to this, Joel and Shannon's is less than six miles away, but it will take us ninety minutes to get there." Frustrated, she put the phone down and looked up. "Oh my God. . . ."

"What? What's wrong?"

Monica pointed out the window toward a ridge in the southeast, less than a half-mile away.

It was on fire.

Luis put his hands over his mouth and shut his eyes.

# Armando 8:45 a.m.

WHEN ARMANDO REGAINED CONSCIOUSNESS, HE FELT warm again, but he was afraid to open his eyes. The burned flesh on his face, arms, and hands, stung, and his nostrils were filled with the stench of smoke and scorched earth.

He knew a different, horrible world surrounded him, and if he could keep his eyes closed, he could keep it at bay for just a moment longer. His mind hovered somewhere between nightmare and reverie. He remembered his wife lying in the pool next to him, and the way she smiled at him at the altar on their wedding day. He remembered his last look into her eyes, and her triumphant smile when she won a game of Scrabble. He remembered her last breath in his ear and taking her hand as they walked down the sidewalk in Bodega Bay.

Armando opened his eyes. What he saw was a world impossible to reconcile with the one he had enjoyed with his family hours before. Everything was gone. Houses and vegetation, gone. The pool where Arielle had bid him goodnight was a 25 x 60 foot rectangle of concrete, filled with the black detritus of a burned world. The air was hauntingly silent: no wind, no birds, no cars in the distance. He stood up. He had no idea what it was like further down the hill or whether Monica and Luis had managed to escape, but he needed to find them. He took a step and realized he was not wearing shoes. He must have lost them in the pool. He walked the perimeter twice before discovering his right tennis shoe floating in the water close enough to the edge that he was able to retrieve it. The left shoe was probably floating underneath the foot-deep pile of debris covering the pool's surface. He wasn't going to get back in the water to look for it.

He returned to Carmen, lay chest down on the warm concrete apron, and plunged his arms into the pool, trying to clear away some of the burnt branches and ash floating around her. Peering through the sooty water, he could just make out a ballet flat on her left foot. Her right foot was bare. Armando removed his pajamas, now filthy and burned through in several places, and slowly crawled back into the cold pool to retrieve the shoe from her foot. He set it gently on the cement. It wouldn't fit, but he could wear it like a slipper.

Shivering, Armando put his pajamas back on, then lowered himself down onto the cement next to his wife. He forced himself to look at her body. He didn't want to leave her there, but he couldn't carry her down the hill. He would be lucky if he made it down himself.

Tears filled his eyes. "I wish you were still here with me," he said. "Would you mind if I borrowed your shoe?" He waited in the silence until he knew with certainty that he had her blessing. Then he picked up the shoe and very carefully slid his foot into it. It would work.

"Thank you, Carmencita," he said. He put his hand on her shoulder and kissed the top of her head. He held his lips to her hair and wept. He wanted to stay here with her. How could he leave her? Suddenly the faces of his family filled his mind, and he understood. She was sending him a message. *You need to go. You need to go for them now.*

Armando knew she was right, of course. She always was. He needed to find Monica, Luis, and Arielle, to make sure their family was okay, and to look out for them. That's what was most important to her right now. He could almost feel her hand on his arm, lifting him, telling him to go and find their family.

He got to his feet, turned in the direction of the road and began walking. His feet squished and sloshed in his mismatched shoes. He slid on ash and rock. Nothing else was left. He passed the place where the gate had been, the gate he'd kicked down so he and Carmen could reach the pool. It was gone, as though it had never existed. He kept walking.

Less than a hundred yards away, he passed the remains of their Chrysler. Nothing was left but the metal frame and even parts of that had melted in the heat. Had they stayed, they would have burned to death. The neighbor's house he and Monica had nearly driven into had been destroyed. Anger rose inside him. He clenched his hands into fists. He stood this way for about a minute then forced himself to turn away. Anger wasn't getting him closer to finding his family. Instead, he thought what a miracle it was that Monica and Luis had woken when they did. Three minutes later, and they would not have made it out. He kept going.

Walking down the hill, he forced himself to think ahead, to keep moving forward, though his body protested. His legs trembled with fatigue, and he was light-headed from lack of oxygen. Even though the air had cleared of smoke, he struggled to breathe. Still, he kept moving.

When his body didn't fight him, his mind did. There were moments when he wanted to just stop, there in the middle of the road, and not feel anything. Especially when he thought of his wife; her face would fill his thoughts and threaten to overwhelm him. He pushed it away and pushed on. His responsibility was with his daughter, her daughter, and her husband. Did they make it down the mountain? Were they safe? Where were they now? Then dark thoughts would intrude, and he wondered how he would tell Monica about her mother. How would he explain those last hours with her? How would the family move forward without her? He pushed on.

Armando marveled at the devastation surrounding him. Nearly everything that could burn had been reduced to ash. Destroyed cars and trucks littered the road. Horses and dogs walked around aimlessly, trying to find where their homes had stood. He came upon the burned-out husk of a tree sprawled across the road, blocking it completely. He stopped. He wondered when it had fallen, and if Luis and Monica had gotten through before it fell. Would it have crushed the Chrysler had they made it this far? Had their choice been the pool or this? Looking at the size of the tree, no one could have gotten past it once it fell. He hadn't seen the remains of an Explorer or Audi on the road, and relief surged within him: Luis, Monica, and Arielle must have gotten through. He would keep searching. Painful as it was, Armando moved off the road to get around the fallen tree. He was grateful for the road's downhill slope; he wasn't sure he had the strength to climb the slightest incline. He rounded a corner and stopped, dumbfounded by what he saw.

A yellow house perched on the side of the hill, completely untouched. Even the roses in the flower beds were perfectly intact. Everything on both sides of the house had been incinerated, but somehow the fire had spared this one home. He stared. What on earth would the owners of that home think when they returned to see theirs was the only house on the street spared from destruction? What would they feel? Or, worse, what if they had perished fleeing the one home that didn't burn?

Armando took a deep breath and forced himself to trudge onward. He saw charred remains of trees and bits of twisted metal inexplicably dumped in the middle of the road by wind or fire or both. Armando climbed over what he could, went around when he had to. He tripped and slid half a dozen times.

Rounding a slight bend in the road, he saw a fire engine. Tears followed joy. He wanted to run, but he couldn't. He tried to wave his arms, but it was too painful. He kept walking, straight down the center of the road, straddling the yellow line to keep him oriented. A fireman saw him and came running up the hill.

"Sir, are you all right?"

Armando nodded, breathless.

Novak peered closely at him. "Is your name Armando?" he asked.

"Yes," Armando said, finding his voice. "How do you know my name?"

Other firefighters looked up and came forward, surprise etched on their faces.

"Your son-in-law was up here trying to find you. I promised him we'd try to reach you and your wife." He paused and then asked, "Armando, where is your wife?"

Armando was not prepared to answer this question. His body slumped. He bowed his head and shook it back and forth slowly. His chest heaved, and he tried, but couldn't stop the tears.

Novak lowered his head and fought his own tears. When Armando was seated in the fire engine, and Novak's men began tending to his burns, Armando finally spoke. "I just lost my best friend," he said. "We've loved each other since we were children . . . and I couldn't save her."

The men listened as Armando sat in their truck and told them what happened to him and his wife. They had spent the entire night moving from one harrowing scene to another, trying to rescue as many people as they could. All night they had dealt with loss and destruction. They were all exhausted. Some felt defeated. As they listened to Armando tell his story, some fought back tears. Others didn't bother, and let the tears, and the stress of the last few hours, fall.

"It's amazing you survived," one of them said.

"I have to live," Armando said. He paused. "I'm still going to have to live, but I have no idea how I'll do it."

# Monica 9:30 a.m.

FORTUNATELY, WE MANAGED TO MAKE IT OFF THE COAST road and onto the southbound freeway before the fire on the ridge could reach us. Luis gripped the steering wheel; his fingers and arms ached from clenching it. Looking at him, I could see the tension running through every muscle. I wondered if either of us would ever feel relaxed again. We were almost back to Joel and Shannon's.

Suddenly his phone rang, and I jumped in my seat. Luis fumbled for his phone.

"Who is it?" I cried.

He looked at the screen. "I don't know," he said and answered. "Hello? . . . Yes. . . . Yes, we'll be right there. Did you—?"

"What? Who was it?" This call was the first we'd received all night, and I could barely contain my impatience.

"That's the fireman I told you about. Jason Novak. He said to meet him right now at Santa Rosa Memorial Hospital."

"Oh my God, they found them! Thank you, God, thank you!" I began to cry. Meeting Novak at the hospital could only mean one thing: he had found them, and they were alive.

"I hope they're okay," he said, exiting the freeway.

"God, I pray they're alive. I don't care about anything else."

He flipped around and took the northbound ramp. We were heading back to Santa Rosa. "They could be in pretty bad shape," he said.

"As long as they're alive."

We were shocked to encounter little traffic on the way to the hospital. Given all the chaos we had seen on the roads over the past few hours, the wide-open freeway stretching before us was strange and eerie. When we finally drove into the hospital parking lot, Luis headed straight for the emergency room entrance. As he pulled up to it, I flung open the door and leaped out. I sprinted inside and nearly slammed into the admitting desk.

"Armando and Carmen Berriz! The firemen brought them here. Where are they?"

If the nurse was off-put by my aggression, she didn't show it. "The firemen haven't brought anyone in this way for a while," she said calmly. "I think they're bringing most people through the main entran—."

I cut her off. "Which way?"

She pointed down the hall, and I bolted that direction. It was another entrance. Through the large glass doors, I could see a fire truck parked in the lot. I ran toward it.

"Do you have my parents?" I shouted to the young firefighter sitting in the back. His face was smudged with ash.

He looked up at me, dazed, then his face contorted. "I'm sorry. I'm so sorry."

*He must be here with someone else,* I thought, turned, and ran back toward the emergency room lobby. In the lobby was Luis. His back was to me, and he was talking to the firefighter I had talked to on the hill. I ran up to them, breathless.

Luis turned. "Papá is inside," he said.

"And Mamá?"

Luis shook his head and began to cry.

I succumbed to the fear and pain I had been struggling against for hours. I started shaking uncontrollably and reached out for Luis. He pulled me toward him. I was barely aware as a nurse directed me, Luis, and Jason Novak into a private room. Luis kept his arms wrapped tightly around me.

I turned to the firefighter. "I have to see Papá."

"They're treating his burns. He's going to be okay, but it takes time." Novak said. "Your father is an amazingly strong man."

I already knew that. My father had been amazing and strong my entire life. Still, I nodded, appreciating his words.

"Do you know what happened?" Luis asked.

Novak nodded. "What your father told us was that their car got hung up on a boulder or something in a flower bed. When they realized they were stuck, they ran back to the house and made it into the pool. They kept submerged for hours, trying to come up only for air, but the heater in the pool blew up, and the water turned cold. They kept moving around, trying to keep as far from the smoke and flames as they could, but they were probably dealing with hypothermia on top of smoke inhalation and burns. Right around dawn, just as the fire was starting to subside, he lost your mom. He said she passed peacefully."

Novak was crying, and his voice cracked as he tried to finish the story my father told him.

"I've got a whole crew of young guys out there. We've been at this monster all night. I can't tell you how bad this is, but me and my crew have never seen anything like it. The devastation is beyond anything I've ever seen. It's incomprehensible. We've been rescuing people all night. We're exhausted. Probably overwhelmed. I

don't know at this point. But what I do know is me and my guys
. . . I . . . ." Novak paused, biting back tears. "What I know is that
I've never been so moved by anyone more than your father. . . .
The same for my crew. I've never seen anything like it. Like him."

Luis was holding my hand, but I didn't feel it. My entire body
had gone numb. I was listening to Novak's words, but I couldn't
hear them. All I heard was, *I should have known they weren't
behind me.*

*I should have made sure they had a phone in the car.*

*I should have made them get in the car with us.*

*I should have felt it. I'm their daughter. I should have been able
to sense that they were in trouble.*

Luis's soft voice cut through my thoughts. "It's not your fault,"
he said.

I looked up at him. He looked so tormented. "It's not yours,
either."

"None of you have any blame for this. Please, please believe this,"
Novak said quickly. "This fire—I've been a firefighter for a long
time, and I've never seen anything like this. Nothing. It's a catastro-
phe—. When they finally figure out—. Well, we can't even go there
until it's contained." He stood up. "I'm sorry, but I have to get back
to the truck. We're still getting calls about other people."

I got to my feet and hugged him. He hugged me back, squeezing tight. Despite the lump in my throat, I managed to say, "Thank
you, Mr. Novak. I can't thank you enough."

He just nodded, then turned and hugged Luis.

"Call me Jason, and take care of your father. You have my
number. Call me if there is anything I can do for you." He briefly
waved and hurried out the door.

A television hung on the wall, and I started watching coverage of the fire while Luis slipped out of the room to call Joel and

Shannon. He came back a few minutes later, and we sat together, stunned, watching Santa Rosa burn down on TV.

Finally, a doctor entered the room. He gave us a weary smile as we jumped to our feet. "Your dad's an impressive man. Amazingly strong. He's going to be fine." The doctor continued, "He has severe burns on his head, on both hands and the left side of his body, but otherwise he's okay. It's going to take a while, but he should make a full recovery."

"Can we see him?" I asked.

The doctor nodded, "Yes, follow me."

We followed him through a couple of long corridors and finally arrived in a room. My dad was awake and caught my eye as soon as we entered. He managed a tiny smile. "I'm sorry I couldn't save her," he said.

I tried to embrace him without hurting him, mindful of the burns on his side and face. "Shh. No, don't say it. I'm sorry, Papá. I'm so sorry," I said.

He patted me on the back and smiled at Luis, who stood behind me. Here was my father, lying in a hospital bed, severe burns over half of his body, and he was comforting me, his little girl. "It's okay," he said. "It's okay, Monica. She's with God now. We had a good life. A very good life. And I'm going to keep living."

# Novak, late afternoon

Captain Jason Novak of CalFire's Sonoma/Lake/ Napa unit had been fighting wildland fires since 1999. After nearly twenty years of experience, he knew the basic arc of putting out a wildfire: anchor the firefighters in position; pinch off the fire's path to prevent it from spreading; contain it. In recent years, due to ongoing droughts in California, fires had grown more extensive and more destructive, and firefighters found themselves prioritizing public safety and rescue over containment. When Novak and his crew arrived on the scene of the Tubbs Fire raging through the hills above Santa Rosa, they knew they were dealing with a fire of monstrous size and strength. He knew he and his crew would be pushed to their physical and emotional limits. He wasn't wrong.

Novak's encounters with Monica and Luis that morning were one of many dramas he and his overburdened men would be thrust into that day. When Armando stumbled down the road at 9:00 in the morning, he and his crew were the only people he knew of within a five-mile radius. Had they not been there, it's unlikely Armando would have survived.

Finding Armando and hearing his story touched Novak's crew in a way he'd never experienced. They found him to be simultaneously heartbreaking and inspiring beyond words, and they were more determined than ever to reach his wife. Once they had tended to his burns, Novak's crew made another attempt to get up the road and find Carmen, but they couldn't maneuver the fire engine past the downed tree. Novak called the police to see if they could get a car up there, but there wasn't one to spare; there was still too much chaos in and around the valley. After checking to make sure there were no reports of any civilians still on the mountain, Novak took Armando to the only remaining open hospital, thirty miles away.

Later that afternoon, he and his crew returned with chainsaws, took the tree apart, and drove up to the end of Crystal Court. The area had been reduced to ash, stripped of any sign of life except for two old oak trees that had somehow stood their ground. At the south end of the lot for 5610 Crystal Court was a pool filled with the black and twisted detritus of the most destructive fire he'd ever faced. He found Carmen's body right where Armando had left her. She looked so peaceful, resting on the steps of the pool, that tears stung his eyes.

"Why is she like that?" one of his younger, less experienced men asked.

"Armando was being as careful as he could with her. He wanted her to be comfortable."

"But she was gone."

"Doesn't matter. When you love someone for an entire lifetime, they're a part of you. Even when they die, they're never really gone. And if you believe that death isn't the end, then you know you'll see them again. When you do, you'll want them to know you did everything you could for them. That you loved them all the way."

# La Familia Eterna

My parents were in Dan's pool for over six hours while the Tubbs Fire raged around them. My father would move her from one side to the other, searching for breathable air. They held onto each other the entire time, and over the hours they spoke sparingly, trying to stay beneath the water as much as they could to avoid the flames overhead.

Move over here. Move over there. Here it comes again. Duck. Keep moving. Keep breathing. Stay alive.

In the end, my mother succumbed to hypothermia and cardiac arrest.

My father spent the night after the fire in our home in Moss Landing. The hospital treated his burns, cleaned him up, covered him in bandages, and less than three hours later, discharged him into our care. They needed the beds for people who were in worse shape than he was. When we left the hospital, the only thing he had with him was a hospital gown and some painkillers. He told me he hadn't been aware of any pain until they began to clean the burns, but the cleaning process was excruciating.

The drive home was long, and he slept through most of it, facilitated by exhaustion and medication. Arielle was quiet, and I was too, trying to comprehend not only what just happened but what would happen next. Luis followed behind us in Arielle's Explorer. There is no game plan for family tragedies. No one has any idea what to do. We'd notified all of our family, and Juan and Andrea, my mother's brother and his wife, had left Bend, Oregon with only the clothes on their backs and were on their way to Moss Landing. Getting through Santa Rosa took them an additional two hours, and further south, on Highway 17, they encountered a closure. What would have been a ten-hour trip took them fifteen.

About two-thirds of the way home, once we were south of San Francisco and driving along the coast, my father woke up and started talking. I tried to convince him to save his strength, but he wanted to talk.

He described parts of their night. He said he understood when my mother had died, and that he felt as if he had died. He said that as the sun rose, a wave of profound, yawning, sadness over-whelmed him, washing his entire life into a massive ocean of darkness. He wasn't sure how long he stood there in the center of the pool with his wife's head resting against his shoulder, but now, driving in the car with us, the wave had passed, the sadness was gone, and there was nothing left inside him. He told us that all of a sudden, the focus of his life, where his spirit and his heart had lived for as long as he could remember, was now a void he couldn't comprehend. When my mother died, he'd not had the strength to lift her out of the pool. He could barely get himself out. His body had begun to cramp up in ways that made him increas-ingly fearful that he too would die. He worried about hypother-mia. He struggled to control his shivering body. He knew he had to get out of the pool. He didn't want to leave my mother behind. Not like this. But he was powerless to do anything else. He had never felt this helpless. The most he could do was guide her body to the steps so it rested in a more secure place and wouldn't float away or become submerged. It took the rest of his strength to lift himself out of the pool and collapse, chest down, cheek down onto the concrete apron. Spent, burned, and alone, he passed out.

He told us all of this and then fell into unconsciousness again. He said nothing more during the drive and remained quiet once we brought him inside and put him to bed. Later, my sister and her partner Kevin, arrived at our house, followed by my brother Armando and his wife, Catherine. I remember nothing else about that night.

The following day Juan and Andrea drove my father to Southern California, where he could receive further medical treatment at the Los Angeles County + USC Medical Center, ninety miles from his home in Apple Valley.

As for his state of mind in the days that followed, I can't write that for him. I know he experienced a series of sensory and emotional states brought on by trauma and grief. Waves of confusion overwhelmed him, compounded by a sense of overwhelming loss. The state of loss, in ways, remains with him, and probably will the rest of his life.

Eventually, acceptance replaced loss. My father wasn't aware of this until it happened, well into the second year of his life without my mother, but for the first time since her death, he could be happy again. God is kind in that way. What I don't ask him about is the loneliness I know he feels. I can't ask because I'm not sure I could stand the answer.

The speed and unexpectedness of losing my mother left me wrung out, exhausted, and anxious. We'd had four games of Words With Friends going when she died. She was winning each game. When the games expired, it was as if precious memories were being yanked away, and I relived losing her all over again.

I screamed at my phone and threw it across the room. All I had left was painful, agonizing loneliness. All I wanted was to feel her, touch her, and hear her voice one more time. One more laugh. One more smile. I wanted a hug. I wanted to feel my mother's arms around me. I wanted to wrap my arms around her. I wanted to say goodbye. I wanted to touch her face. I wanted to hear her voice. I wanted her to console me like she did when I was younger.

Instead, I got nightmares.

Or more accurately, a nightmare, since for nearly two years it was always the same. It began with me getting in the car and driving down Dan's driveway and ended with me realizing I don't know where I'm going, and my parents are no longer behind me. I am outside the car, surrounded by flames. The nightmare felt like a violation because during the day, I was relatively okay. I had come to terms with myself, and with God, and with my powerlessness to have that night turn out any differently. And on the days when I couldn't quite understand or accept what happened, I could at least rationalize it. But then the night would come and with it, the nightmare.

One day, an associate of Luis's who'd faced a particularly painful and challenging experience of her own revealed that after trying a number of paths to get past the pain, she'd been directed to a shaman. Meeting the shaman, she said, was a profound experience that allowed her to move forward with her life. She thought this shaman might be able to help me.

I was game. I had nothing to lose. I had sold my business because I couldn't deal with the daily responsibilities and stress of managing it anymore. My days disappeared from underneath me, lost in a fog of despair and grief. Days became weeks, and weeks became months. It had been a year and a half since my mom had died, and I was barely functioning, crippled by loss and regret.

The shaman's name was Alana. Her area of expertise was in helping families find acceptance and forgiveness. In particular, she worked with people who wanted to reach out to deceased loved ones with whom they'd had difficult or challenging experiences in life. When I called, I didn't know if this fit my situation, but I was desperate.

When I heard Alana's voice on the phone, she spoke with a calmness and clarity, and with a careful directness that I wasn't expecting. Soon I was telling her everything that happened the night of the fire, and in the year and a half since. She listened patiently and gently asked probing questions. Then she asked if I was ready to reach out to my mother now, right now.

"Yes. I am," I said.

She asked me to put the phone on speaker, then lay down on my back and get comfortable. I put my phone face up on the nightstand next to my bed, then awaited more instructions. She walked me through a deep breathing exercise, putting me in a deeply meditative state. Next, she asked me to visualize my breathing in square shapes. This visualization provided a structure and an even path. Up, then over, then down, in repeating squares. One measure after another. One breath at a time, progressing from one column to the next. As she guided me through this pattern, my mind and body slowed, and I became more aware. I could feel my blood pressure change, my heartbeat slowing down, and my blood moving through my veins and my body. My extremities began to tingle, and the sensation worked its way up my limbs.

It was beginning to feel like we were performing a ritual together, even though she wasn't in the room with me. After a few minutes of this, she began beating a drum, which had a low-sounding, bass tone. It sounded as if she was beating it with a stick, not her hand, creating the rhythm of a heartbeat. After a few minutes of this, I heard whisking sounds coming from her end. Lying on my bed with my eyes closed, my arms at my side and legs at rest, I began to feel a kind of electric surge grow within me, which at first gave me chills then became a warmth of pure energy pulsing through me. Wild images flooded my mind— abstract images—the meanings of which were unclear to me, but imparted a sense of almost tactile warmth and safety. As I continued to breathe, the images solidified into a bright and unmistakable sense of my mother. I had no doubt I was in her presence. I couldn't see her face, but I could see it was her. I could feel her.

"Mamá!" I said out loud.

The whisking sound continued, and several seconds passed before Alana spoke again. "Monica, what is your mother's name?"

"Carmen."

"Okay, good. Your mother, Carmen, is with us now. She's here present with us. Talk to her."

I began to cry.

Then I began to talk. To my mother. Through my tears. Some of the words I wanted to say came out of my mouth, and looking back, there were others I simply felt without saying aloud. It didn't really matter, to me at least, because I was talking with my mom again.

I told my mom I was sorry. Sorry that I couldn't help her. Sorry I couldn't get back to her. Sorry I never got to hold her that night. That she never got to hold me. That I didn't have the opportunity to look into her eyes and feel her warmth one last time.

I repeated these apologies over and over, sobbing through the words. Then my mother's warmth embraced me, and it kept growing until my breathing smoothed out, and I stopped crying. Then I told her I missed her.

I missed so many things about her, but more than anything, I said, I just missed her.

I told her I wanted to hug her.

And finally, I asked her if she could ever forgive me.

My mother laughed gently and embraced me. Her breath brushed my cheek as she laughed softly and held me close to her.

While she held me, she spoke these words to me: *It all happened the way it was supposed to happen. You need to grow beyond this. You need to live your life, Monica. You have love, and a family, and you will be fine. I am always with you.*

My mother's hug that day is, without exception, the single most incredible sensation I have ever experienced in my life. Somehow, she knew this was exactly what I needed—that on countless nights since the night she'd died, I had prayed for her to hold me in her arms again.

I was still experiencing this hug when a bright light eclipsed everything else, and I sensed it was time for her to go.

"Thank you," I said. "Thanks for everything, but I understand you need to go. I'm okay. I am okay. I understand it's time. Time for you to be with Jesus. We'll be okay. I love you, Mamá."

Like my parents, I'm a Catholic. Unlike my parents, I wouldn't consider myself a devout Catholic, at least for most of my adult life. I do not know why I said she needed "to be with Jesus," but that's what I said to her. She, too, sensed she needed to go, and while I still could not see her face, I felt a tear fall from her cheek onto mine. Then she let go of her embrace, and her image began to disappear in the light. As it did, I became aware of Alana's drum beating again, and as my mother's presence receded, Alana's drum grew louder.

Just before my mother faded into the light, she looked over her shoulder at me and smiled.

I lay on my bed, alone, and listened to the drum through the phone on my pillow. I was trying to absorb what had just happened when the tears began to flow. I'd cried a lot since the morning of

October 9th, 2017, more than I thought anyone could ever cry, but the tears I cried on my bed that afternoon were different. Those other tears had been born of grief, fear, regret, sorrow, shame, and millions more for a million other things.

These were tears of absolution and joy. These tears were cathartic. I understood that it was time for me to move forward. My mother had told me so.

I must have cried for ten minutes before I heard Alana say my name softly, "Monica?"

"Yes, I'm here. I'm okay. Give me a minute, please."

She did. Then she said, "Your mother has returned to the light. Would you like to talk?"

"No. I mean, can we speak later? Another time? I need to absorb this."

"Yes. Of course. Let me know when you're ready. Can I tell you one thing before I let you go?"

"Yes, please."

"Your mother is in a good place. She is at peace with God, she is happy, and she is close to you."

"I know. Thank you, Alana."

She hung up. The entire call lasted about thirty minutes.

# La Familia Continua

Two years after the fire, in October 2019, I drove to Apple Valley to help my father pack up his home. My parents' home. He had decided to move to Moss Landing, and a day after he made that decision, a house came on the market two blocks down the street from ours and closer to the beach. In one sense, I was very happy about this, ecstatic even, but the joy was bittersweet. Yes, my father was moving closer to us. Yes, we would get to spend more time with him. Yes, I was overjoyed with the certainty that his closeness to Luis was a significant factor in his decision. But none of that joy could remove the slashing truth that my mother wasn't going to be with him.

I was concerned about the emotions around this event—not only mine and my father's, but those of my brother and sister. Within months of the fire, my father decided he no longer wanted any of my mother's things in the house. He also didn't want much of anything else in it either. He didn't want to have to dust, clean, or polish things, including family photos, my mother's keepsakes, souvenirs from their travels, and all of her clothing. My sister and I got some of the clothing we were interested in, but he gave away a number of things to Goodwill we would have rather kept for ourselves, which was heartbreaking to both of us.

Much to my surprise and considerable relief, the experience of packing the house was a positive one. Instead of feeling a sense of loss, every time I picked something up, I was reminded of a pleasant memory associated with it. Each touch made me feel warm inside, and I enjoyed holding things up to my father and telling him what I remembered about it: where it came from, who brought it into our house in Glendale, and when. Most of the day went like that, and it was fantastic to revisit our family's history in this tactile and emotional way.

The best part was the bookcases. My parents always had a lot of books in the house, and they had enormous floor to ceiling bookcases. One of them held a wooden bust of Cervantes, which they kept next to a beautiful leather-bound copy of *Don Quixote* (in Spanish, of course). I cannot count the number of times I removed this bust, and the book next to it, and carefully dusted these gorgeous treasures as a young girl. It reminded me of when my sister and I were little, and we shared the chores. What usually comes to my mind when I think about those years are the arguments we had as children, which were frequent and frequently fierce, but that afternoon I remembered the fun we used to have touching the precious things in our parents' home and learning about them.

I also found the beautiful linens my mother had collected from around the world, which she would use at parties. Like everything in her life, she'd organized these linens by color and fabric and hung them carefully in a closet. She had more than a dozen full sets. I handled them gingerly, recalling faces, names, and moments I hadn't thought of in years. Emotions were strong that day, but more than anything else, I was proud to be my parents' daughter.

As I helped my father pack up the house that weekend, I realized this would be the first time since boarding school that he would be moving to a new place to live on his own. In college, he lived with his parents, and by the time he graduated, he and my mother were already married. He'd only lived in three homes in fifty-eight years, and all had been organized, and managed, by my mother.

So, I did what my mother would have done: I took charge of everything. I told him what I needed him to do, and he did it. This was a huge relief to me. He wasn't quiet, morose, or maudlin. Rather, he responded with the enthusiasm of a man genuinely looking forward to starting a new chapter in his life. He told me he was grateful for the help and expressed his gratitude by being happy and following my directions to a tee. His spirits were light, and his excitement about moving forward was contagious.

Toward the end of the weekend, after we had packed up nearly everything in the house. I was standing alone in the living room, taking in the strangeness of its emptiness. My father entered the room, holding a wine-colored box.

"I want you to have this, Monica. Your mother would have wanted you to have it."

It was my mother's old Scrabble set. The one we used as children. The one my mother and I played countless games on. The box was well-worn but intact. I took it from him almost reverently and held it for the first time in decades.

Games were an important part of my mother's life, and they became an important part of mine. She was a world-class volleyball player in her youth, and we still play a lot of board games in our home. We didn't play Scrabble anymore; instead, Rummikub, Farkle, and Yahtzee rule. I win a lot, but not like my mom did. I know there's a metaphor there, that I've replaced the meticulous, word-based games I'd once played with my mother and loved ones for games based on random rolls of the dice.

"Oh my God, Papá! Thank you."

"No, thank you, Monica."

He turned away from me and took his cell phone out of his pocket and started tapping it. My father delighted in his new-found ability to stream any song he could think of from the palm of his hand and listen to it on wireless speakers spread throughout the house. He had insisted we pack them last so we could listen to music while we packed.

He looked up at me and smiled. "Ever since this song came out, it has always reminded me of your mother."

From the first notes of the guitar, I recognized The Hollies' "Long Cool Woman (In a Black Dress)."

My father started dancing around the room, slowly, but with evident joy. When the bass and drums kicked in, he cranked it up and smiled at me.

I could see him mouthing the words as he moved to the beat. He knew the lyrics, which surprised me, and I doubt he ever really thought about them very carefully, but I understood why this song reminded him of his wife and my mother. To me, him, and to everyone who knew her, she was a woman who had it all, had it all, had it all.

# Epilogue

IN OCTOBER 2017, OVER ONE HUNDRED SEVENTY WILD-fires, including twenty-one major fires, burned across Northern California in what CalFire called the Fire Siege. The fires raged for weeks before being fully contained. Forty-four people, including my mother, were killed.

Pacific Gas & Electric was responsible for almost all of the devastation. Blown transformers, deferred maintenance, and their failure to keep trees trimmed and away from power lines as required by law caused the fire siege. The company has filed for bankruptcy and settled claims worth billions of dollars since.

In November 2018, the Camp Fire in Northern California killed eighty-five and wiped out the town of Paradise. Faulty PG&E equipment was determined to be the cause of this fire.

In November 2018, the Woolsey Fire in Southern California burned 97,000 acres, destroyed 1,643 structures, and killed three people. Although this fire is still under investigation, it is speculated that South California Edison equipment was associated with its ignition. Seminole Springs Mobile Home Park in the Santa Monica Mountains lost 110 out of 215 homes. My sister's home was among them. To date, homeowners have been unable to rebuild, and Seminole Springs Mobile Home Park needs $10 million to repair its infrastructure.

The state of California passed legislation allowing PG&E to pass on the costs of the fires and the resulting lawsuits directly to their customers, the very people whose homes they destroyed, and whose families they killed.

PG&E continues its business practices. California continues to burn. Lives continue to be lost. People continue to suffer.

On March 23, 2020, PG&E pleaded guilty to eighty-four counts of involuntary manslaughter in the Northern California fires alone.


AFTER MY FATHER TOLD ME THE DETAILS OF WHAT HAP-pened to them that night, I spent countless hours every day for weeks on end, imagining what was going through my mother's mind.

What might she have said if she could still speak, and what would she want my father to know? What would she want me and my sister and brother to know?

I'll never know, but I want to believe that when my mother opened her eyes and saw my father's face in front of hers, she believed he was more handsome now than he had been when he was young. That she loved this face, lined with age, but filled with strength. I believe that being held in his arms made her comfortable and eased her mind at what was approaching. Slowly, though, I believe she became aware of another presence, another warmth, another love, enveloping them both. It warmed her through, and as it did, she knew it was time to go. She looked at her husband, and her eyes told him what she could not say with words. My father, in telling me what happened to them that night, says the look in my mother's eyes was a look he had never seen before. How could he? She had never told him goodbye before. Then he says a warmth flushed through her skin into his hands and radiated outward, warming his chest. I believe as the warmth around her grew more intense, she knew with a surge of peace that this wasn't goodbye. She would see him again, and they would be together forever: *Hasta que estemos juntos de nuevo, mi amor.*

# Acknowledgments

THE MOST BEAUTIFUL GIFTS ARE BORN FROM THE ASHES OF a tragic event. It is with much gratitude I acknowledge just a few of the many individuals that reached out and made a huge difference.

Jason Novak, Firefighter, thank you for your heroism.

USC Burn Center, notably, Nurse Christine, who performed the first debridement, thank you for your compassion.

The Red Cross, thank you for your support and resources, including Post Traumatic Syndrome counseling.

Father Frank Ferrante, thank you for your prayers and counsel after the accident.

Father Jim Stehley, thank you and the St. Jude parish in Westlake for including us in your Family.

Marianne Kirkpatrick, Joan Anderson, and Lou Weaver, thank you for volunteering your time to take care of my father's wounds.

Joel and Shannon Taatjes, thank you for your friendship and love.

Dan Brown, thank you for your love, and the hours you put into looking for my ring in the ashes of your home's remains.

Jane James, thank you for your enjoyable company at a time when it was much needed.

Alan Wayne, thank you for empowering my mom at United Airlines. May you always rest in peace.

Alana Blusol, thank you for clearing that which did not belong.

Mark Rudio, thank you for bringing life to the idea.

Jay Christopher, thank you for your brilliance and hard work.

Jose and Adelita Pose, thank you for your unwavering, life-long friendship.

My dad's siblings, Albert Berriz and Berta Berriz, thank you for your profoundly healing efforts.

My brother and sister-in-law, Armando and Catherine Berriz, thank you for your strength in faith and family.

My sister, Carmen Berriz Meissner, and Kevin Kiesau, thank you for our relationship, which I cherish deeply.

My daughter, Arielle Lysacek, thank you for giving me purpose.

My mom's brother and sister-in-law, Juan and Andrea Caldentey, a very special thank you for graciously and meticulously caring for my dad's wounds, physical and spiritual.

My husband, Luis E. Ocon, thank you for saving us.

My dad, Armando Berriz, thank you for relentlessly battling despite overwhelming odds. Your strength and determination are unparalleled.

# About the Author

Monica Berriz-Ocon, a first-generation Cuban American, was born in 1964 to Armando and Carmen Berriz. Monica and her two siblings, Carmen Teresa who is older by 11 months, and Armando Juan, who is younger by four years, were reared in Glendale, California together at the hand of their maternal grandmother, Carmela Caldentey. Traditional Hispanic customs were respected and upheld in their household, including speaking only Spanish as a result of her grandmother refusing to learn English.

Monica graduated from Glendale High School in 1982 and went to Art Center College of Design in Pasadena, California, to study Advertising. After completing her studies in 1987, Monica became a Marketing Manager for various companies. At the age of 26, Monica gave birth to her only natural born daughter, Arielle Lysacek, and moved to Newport Beach for work. There they both lived together for 17 years until Arielle left, having graduated from Newport Harbor High School in 2009, to play volleyball for the University of North Carolina, at Greensboro.

Later that same year, Monica reconnected with her husband-to-be, Luis E. Ocon, and moved up to Monterey County to live with him. There, Monica uses her marketing talents part-time to help grow her husband's Chiropractic office. She also invests in real estate and entrepreneurial ventures.

Monica's primary focus and devotion is to her family: Wife to Luis Ocon, mother to Arielle Lysacek, step-mother to Christian and Gian Ocon, and mother-in-law to Dennis Zmijewski. Her new purpose includes her first two grandchildren, Amelia and Brayden.

www.ingramcontent.com/pod-product-compliance
Lightning Source LLC
Chambersburg PA
CBHW031127090426
42738CB00008B/1002

* 9 7 8 1 9 4 7 9 6 6 4 1 3 *